FIRST FIRE, THEN BIRDS

Also by H. L. Hix

POETRY
Incident Light *
Legible Heavens *
God Bless *
Chromatic *
Shadows of Houses *
Surely As Birds Fly
Rational Numbers
Perfect Hell

ARTISTS' BOOKS AND LIMITED EDITIONS
This Translucent Tissue (artist's book by Judi Ross)
The Last Hour (artist's book by Egidijus Rudinskas)
Intellectual Pleasures (limited edition by Aralia Press)

TRANSLATIONS
Jüri Talvet, *Estonian Elegy: Selected Poems*, trans. with the author
Juhan Liiv, *The Mind Would Bear No Better*, trans. with Jüri Talvet
On the Way Home: An Anthology of Contemporary Estonian Poetry, trans. with Jüri Talvet
Jüri Talvet, *A Call for Cultural Symbiosis*, trans. with the author
Eugenijus Ališanka, *City of Ash*, trans. with the author

ANTHOLOGIES
New Voices: Contemporary Poetry from the United States
Wild and Whirling Words: A Poetic Conversation *

THEORY AND CRITICISM
As Easy As Lying: Essays on Poetry *
Understanding William H. Gass
Understanding W. S. Merwin
Spirits Hovering Over the Ashes: Legacies of Postmodern Theory
Morte d'Author: An Autopsy

* Also published by Etruscan Press

FIRST FIRE, THEN BIRDS
OBSESSIONALS 1985-2010

H. L. HIX

Etruscan Press

Etruscan Press
Wilkes University
84 West South Street
Wilkes-Barre, PA 18766

W WILKES UNIVERSITY
www.etruscanpress.org

Library of Congress Cataloging-in-Publication Data

Hix, H. L.
First fire, then birds : obsessionals,
1985-2010 / H.L. Hix. -- 1st ed.
    p. cm.
    ISBN 978-0-9819687-4-2 (hardcover)
    I. Title.
    PS3558.I88F57 2010
    811'.54--dc21
    2010019107

Cover photograph: Michael Stringer, Pleurosigma (marine diatoms)
Design by Tara Caimi

Acknowledgments

The book's epigraph is quoted from Andrew Joron, *The Cry at Zero*. The epigraph to "Fire" comes from Ludwig Wittgenstein, *Zettel*, and to "Birds" from Joy Williams, *Breaking and Entering*.

I am grateful to the editors of the following journals for giving first publication to the new poems included in this book: *Margie* ("Child of Their Old Age"), *Pleiades* ("Though What Falls . . . "), *Poetry* ("Even Be It Built of Boards . . . "), *Serving House* ("Calendologium"), *Washington Square* ("Intercourse amounts to . . . "). "Valediction" was created for, and published in, *The Burden of the Beholder*, a collaboration between poets and artist David Armstrong, edited by Jane Hilberry and published by The Press at Colorado College.

This book revises and reconfigures portions of books first published by Gibbs Smith, SUNY Press, Truman State University Press, and Etruscan Press. I thank those publishers for their generous support of my work. "This Particular Eden" and the poems in "So I Might Have Your Company in Hell" were published first in *Perfect Hell* (Gibbs Smith, 1996); "Orders of Magnitude" and "Figures" in *Rational Numbers* (Truman State Univ. Press, 2000); "Thistle, Clover, Rape," "A Study of Thermodynamics," and "A Manual of Happiness" in *Surely As Birds Fly* (Truman State Univ. Press, 2002); "The God of Restlessness," "The God of Window Screens and Honeysuckle," "The Law," and "The Prophets" in *Shadows of Houses* (Etruscan, 2005); "Remarks on Color," "Eighteen Maniacs," and "The Well-Tempered Clavier" in *Chromatic* (Etruscan, 2006); "All the One-Eyed Boys in Town," "Material Implication," "Star Chart for the Rainy Season," and "Synopsis" in *Legible Heavens* (Etruscan, 2008); "Listings" in *Spirits Hovering Over the Ashes* (SUNY Press, 1995); "Gently Omitted" and "Toward a Prodigal Logic" in *As Easy As Lying* (Etruscan, 2002); and "First Term" in *God Bless* (Etruscan, 2007).

The second section of this book, "Birds," represents a redaction of my attempts to "write over" biblical books. As with the original biblical books, each poem is intended to stand on its own, but because the derivation of my poem from a biblical original will be more obvious in some cases than in others, let me not be coy about identifying each. "This Particular Eden" relates to Genesis 1 & 2, "Child of Their Old Age" to Genesis 18, "Listings" to Leviticus, "Less Said" to Numbers, "Toward a Prodigal Logic" to Deuteronomy, "First Term" to Kings, "Figures" to Ecclesiastes, "Star Chart for the Rainy Season" to the Song of Songs, "A Study of Thermodynamics" to Lamentations, "A Manual of Happiness" to Job, "The Prophets" to the minor prophets, "Synopsis" to the gospels, including various non-canonical gospels, "The Letters" to the letters, and "Calendologium" to the Revelation of Ezra. In "First Term," the poems designated by a month are constructed entirely of passages from speeches, executive orders, and other public statements of George W. Bush; the "interleaves" reformulate arguments from the communications of Osama bin Laden.

The books in which this work first appeared include additional apparatus (attributions, dedications, and other records of indebtedness) that I have minimized here, though my debts only increase in number and in degree. My debt to Phil Brady grows with each book, and my debt to Kate Northrop with each day.

Table of Contents

FIRST FIRE, THEN BIRDS

Language is not predicated on the existence of meaning, but is an unpredictable outcome of a world that produced first fire, then birds.

FIRE

Compare the phenomenon of thinking with the phenomenon of burning.

Even Be It Built of Boards Planed by Hand and Joined Without Nails, Yet May a Barn Burn

The three men now stood satisfied, arms crossed,
joking among themselves, but only moments before
they hadn't been laughing. It had taken all three
to bind the struggling man. First, to limit his movement,
they had duct-taped his wrists together behind his back:
for that, one man had held his legs and another had pinned him,
one hand on each shoulderblade and one knee on his head,
at his left temple, grinding his right cheek and eye into
the dust and straw and dried shit that formed the floor of the barn.
First they bound his wrists, then his ankles. Then it got easier.
More tape over his mouth, wound all the way around his head,
three full loops, much more than was necessary, which was one thing
they were laughing about, the two bigger men making fun
of the smaller one, who had done that part of the binding.
Then they'd bound him down on the mattress, again with the tape.

The bound man continued to struggle, but once the tape
denied him movement he felt as if he were thinking clearly,
as if his panic had lifted, resistance become
mere obligation. He thought surely the tape would run out,
but they had another roll, just in case. He noticed
the new order—head first this round—when it came to the mattress.
One man would lift one end just off the dirt, enough
for another to wrap the tape, which cursed coming off the roll
in what the man construed as sympathy, all the way
around the mattress in loops that included his head and neck,
then the same process at the other end,
all the way around the mattress and his ankles.

They couldn't figure how to get the tape around his torso
because it was so near the middle of the mattress.

The bound man found himself wanting to help, but of course
he couldn't speak, and anyway they didn't need his advice.
His hands bound behind his back and against the mattress meant
his feet and head, and most of all his neck, were plenty
to keep him from getting loose and grabbing one of their guns.

The bound man's life didn't pass before him in summary,
exactly, but he did see things now that in all these years
he hadn't noticed. The wiring, for instance.
He thought it must have been his own father who'd wired the barn
with that odd blend of pride and makeshift half-competence
that showed up in all his father'd made, himself not least.
One bare bulb bragging from the highest joist
about its white porcelain fixture, but better, really,
at casting long shadows than at lighting the place,
though if the three men would just leave him alone, he thought,
he'd be able to count up all the birds' nests and speculate
on where swallows had built before there were barns.
The wire ran from switchbox to fixture in straight lines
and right angles, through half-inch galvanized surely intended
for plumbing but good, too, for frustrating the rats.

It was the short man, the one who'd done all the taping, who then
poured kerosene across the mattress and over the man,
soaking his clothes, making sure to splash some into his eyes.
No one else noticed, but he spelled out FUCK with the kerosene.
Or anyway swung his arms in that pattern. That was when
they could relax a little, the three men, and start their joking,
once the kerosene was poured. One tall man slapped his forehead:
"You brought matches, right?" "Matches?," the other replied,
furrowing his brow and patting his pockets,
and both laughed out loud. Even the short man smiled.

Barns burn, it turns out, just the way you'd think
if you thought about it, hay fast and hot,
siding lighting the roof and the flooring of the loft,
all the slender strips of wood, with the few parts *not* tinder—
the frame, the beams and joists—starting last and lasting longest.
But that's not what the mattress-bound man's great-great-grandfather
had thought about, its someday burning, as he built the barn.
He had a daughter to worry about, and a wife
big with what he thought might be a boy. And weather,
and a dozen cows. Plenty to fret more immediate
than which fuck-up would later taint his bloodline
and preside over the decay, finally
inviting the sacrifice, of what he had built to last.

Barns burn like bonfires built for the burning,
stacked just so by one mortal for the next.
They burn best at night, whether or not communicants
travel up and down billows lit silver from above,
red from below. And whether or not three men
have stopped among sycamores on the rise just opposite
and turned for a moment to admire their handiwork.

So I Might Have Your Company in Hell

I will start by telling you an ancient legend

She smiled when she passed him. He started when
she smiled, having passed her more often than
he wanted to remember. He smiled when
he passed her until he learned to look down.
She smiled a smile that was no expression.
She smiled when he started, just like someone
he wanted to remember. She looked down,
he remembered, like she was no one.
She was no one. She passed him. He looked down.
He wanted to remember her, but when
she passed him, smiling without expression,
he was no one. He learned to look down.
He wanted to remember. She passed. When
she smiled at him his face began to burn.

The vagina is a sexual crematorium

The lesson is:
there is no lesson, no secret,
nothing to understand. The lesson is:
what can be done in a back seat
can be done against a tree.
Who has screamed will bite.
From anything you can see
but not see into, something can see out.
The lesson is: what lets you enter it
stays hungry.
What you can arouse you cannot placate.
Not every bruise is an injury.
What is not death is a wait.
Follow me.

On rising from bed, obliterate the print of your body

On rising from bed, obliterate the print of your body.
On walking through sand, erase the prints of your feet.
Walk through sand if you must return to the sea.
On combustion, turn white hot.
On petrifying, begin uniform isotope decay.
On waking from a dream, dissipate into the night.
Wake from a dream if you can refuse the next day.
On impact, accelerate.
No epiphany can compensate a disappearance.
Well ended matches well begun.
A thousand flights, but a feather falls only once.
If you must be water, be rain.
Stare at oncoming lights and you'll die in a trance.
If you must sleep, do not be seen.

The spindle turns on the knees of necessity

The cold call of cold calling cold
follows itself to the moon,
to the storm-edge of storm, to the folds of fold
in the shrouds of the fallen-too-soon.
The call of cold to the never-held,
the sung-over and one-by-one,
follows the moon to that world where this world
pulls always, pulls all, and pulls down.
From high to higher, from sharp to celeste,
from already over to barely begun,
from once to after, from east to east,
the call's cold turnings call what cold cannot turn:
the knees of the knees of the must
thrust between not yet and never again.

The last crows whose cries are audible here

In this cottonwood crows condense at dusk,
saturate night, evaporate at daybreak.
They pose the questions one knows not to ask,
stand answers one does not know how to take.
They console bare limbs for lost leaves. Their flights
lilt lines in verse translations of the snow
into a tongue, inscrutable by light,
that no diurnal mind will ever know.
Their names are given by the wind, their one
master, whose calls to them are audible
among their own: *Wherefore, Nothing, In vain,*
Burning burning burned, Lost, Impalpable,
Map of the abyss, Listen my love listen,
Illegible, Hardly, The unchained fall.

The possibility of all situations

I may kill. You should know this about me.
A razor in the night, without warning.
Objects contain the possibility
of all situations. States of being
embrace all imaginable events.
Any life, any pair of lives, harbors
every death. The succession of presents
comprehends all foreseeable futures.
I have it in me to be a galaxy
or one leaf on the frond of a fern.
I may have been light in a sanctuary
kindled by a rose window, become cairn
older than the woods it renders holy.
I may flood or avalanche. I may burn.

As though the weather were bad in the world of sexuality

The man with the crooked dick shines his shoes.
The woman with one arm takes off her brassiere.
The man straps a dildo between his knees.
The woman stands on her head on a chair.
She wants him to kneel. He wants her to scream.
He bloodies her lip as a compromise.
She wants want at work. He wants want at home.
He curses and curses. She cries and cries.
He likes to pull her hair. She likes to bite.
He always has to be last to undress.
With someone you love, at this time of night,
it's hard to distinguish kick from caress.
The clockface would be the room's only light
did not their bodies at contact fluoresce.

Definite descriptions

The choice divorced from decision.
The year with too few and too many days.
The juxtaposition
the result of which is always
the perfect elision.
The thing that now neither of them says.
The passion to consummate their destruction.
The color in her eyes reflected in his.
The Earth Mother's granddaughter, Rose Rose Rose,
the water she bathes with, where she nests,
what she shows
the men she ingests.
The one man still living who knows
the difference in size between her breasts.

The pine-tree seems to listen

The pine seems to listen, the fir to wait
while its insects insist on the serifs
that finish, embellish, punctuate
the cyrillic calligraphy, the cursives
they carve across a cellulose tablet
lined, circled, curtained with the annual
residues of defense against what
will not nourish, against what cannot fill.
A script in a patois parasites know,
a proof that we die, we die, we die
and are eaten from the inside, although
not in that order. A long eulogy
in praise of the patient, hyloid, hollow,
of those who are eaten, those who supply.

Is the absence of feeling a feeling?

Suppose this pain I now suffer exists
in some body not my own, in some world
far distant from me. Suppose it consists
in not feeling pain. Take it as culled,
only an after-image, the wooden chair
still rocking after someone has risen,
the photographer's shadow in a picture.
Say my absence creates no contradiction,
that this pain exists and can exist only
when I am having no experience:
the one taking the late-night call is not me,
I will not drive all night, not try to make sense
of why this pain is not pain, so intensely,
why its effect must be felt at a distance.

A number of fragile and brittle things

The heart, of course, famous for the ease
with which it gets broken; porcelain,
tissue, crystal; wings of butterflies;
old photos; a fossil skeleton.
But also the long ant trail of days
that follows itself (no one, no one,
no one) always to its own carcass
of yellow love letters and shed skin.
Dried tongues of distant relatives,
those pressed leaves passed on, generation
to generation. And forgiveness,
the glass wall into which we run
to shatter ourselves into something else
our children's feet will cut themselves on.

So many rats, so many florins

So many rats, so many florins,
so many numbers to call.
So many days, so many worlds since
the sky started slowly to fall.
So many quarks, so many superstrings,
so much loose change in the car.
So many hopes, so many underthings
strewn from bed back to the door.
So few crowned lemurs left outside zoos,
so few sea turtles at all.
So few so often make so little use
of so much so seldom so small.
So few exits make it hard to refuse
the window, the window, the wall.

Their consent to make themselves one person

The man with the crooked dick rakes the leaves.
The woman with one arm dons an old dress.
The man wipes the grease from his face on his sleeves.
The woman plucks three dark hairs from her face.
He fills the compost pile. She fills the trash.
He wipes the shit from his shoes on the grass.
He scratches his crotch. She plucks one more lash.
The tissue she kisses will wipe his ass.
The man leaves his jacket outside with the rake.
When he comes inside she closes her door.
She says he smells bad, he says she looks sick.
He pinches her nipple, she bites his ear.
He calls her a shit, she calls him a prick.
But they spend the next hour on the bathroom floor.

While it was in fact raining

While it was in fact raining, while chill wind
beat a loose gutter against one eave,
while a blundering god failed to descend
as more than water, as what one could believe
even in this dream, while sheet lightning
drew the breath between shaping its lips
and the coughing of its monotonous song,
a woman pulled her jeans over her hips,
her sweater over her head, her hair
out of her sweater to let it fall down
her back and over her shoulders, where
an hour ago the dreamer's hands had been,
and opened the door to her dream, its air,
scored redolent by such rough rain, certain.

Countless dark bodies are to be inferred near the sun

Near the sun, no farther than the distance
from one mind to another, no farther
than conjugation from detumescence,
love from loss, fulfillment from desire,
are bodies darker than the insistence
of insects on inviolate order,
darker than increase, loss, senescence,
darker than a moonless night in winter.
They skim in a tight albatross orbit
or whirl in tiny epicycles
one around another. They burn or melt
spontaneously. In their rare collisions
they do not fuse. More impermanent
than, and as invisible as, ourselves.

Emptiness gets imprisoned in bodies

The man with the crooked dick wipes his nose.
The woman with one arm washes her hair.
The man wipes his armpits with her dirty clothes.
The woman sticks bubble gum under his chair.
He likes her sweaty. She likes him clean.
He does forty pushups while she takes her bath.
She wants a puppy. He wants a machine.
She measures with whimpers. He measures with math.
He thinks about women he knew in school.
She thinks about men she knows at work.
Her present is empty. His past is not full.
If he would come she could finish her book.
They kick off the blanket but it does not fall
until he bites the pillowcase and they quake.

1 is the point, 2 the line, 3 the triangle, 4 the pyramid

5 is the praying mantis,
6 the sunning cat stretched across a sidewalk.
7 is where the cat was
that disappeared before you looked back.
8 is the tiny piece
of another world in the mirror of a passing car,
9 the same cat somewhere else
eyes closed, tongue stroking and stroking its fur.
10 is the end of summer:
the way leaves in the wind sound when they are brittle,
that they turn black in the gutter,
what the sun warms from its new angle,
how crushed crabapples clutter
sidewalks with their bloodstains and sweet rotting smell.

The bones of its mother are bright eyes

The bones of its mother are bright eyes
and the wings of its father one clay fist.
Its mother sings the moon across the skies
its father wears the sun around his wrist.
Its sister is its brother in disguise
its brother is its sister with a twist:
when she loses organs and limbs he cries,
when he loses his life she will be missed.
It knows the names of all the stars by heart
in the fractal tongue they sang to it at birth
but fashioned an argot that could report
to Vacuum what it means to be the fourth
of three children metamorphosed into light
careening irreversibly from earth.

The fact which I am now observing

Here is my body, farther from itself
than from those curtains or that mantel-piece,
or than my mind from the books on that shelf,
farther than the wish from the fact of release
in cooing spirits caged in human bodies
neither like nor wholly unlike my own,
from which my separation could not increase,
with which I could not be any more one.
Often have I perceived human bodies
make the sound of slow steps in the stairwell,
brush the gauze curtains, crouch in the fireplace,
creak over floorboards when the house was still,
and thought them my own bodies, and thought I was
the inhuman one, the immaterial.

I go with him to hell

A week ago you could have helped me.
You could have told me that it would happen
and when and why (after nearly forty
years of marriage), and that there would be no one
with us to help and that it would not be
in sleep with a blissful smile on his face
but falling, his head hitting the TV,
and writhing, face contorted, in his own piss.
A week ago you could have told me
what it would feel like to drive alone
behind the ambulance, that eternity
starts in a line of cars stopped by a train,
that at the mouth of hell when you would pay
with your soul for a parking place you find none.

This morally neutralized domain of intercourse

The man with the crooked dick strikes a match.
The woman with one arm breaks into flame.
The man finds a bird's skull and wants to play catch.
The woman hears the skull calling her name.
He looks out the window. She looks in the door.
He crushes a spider onto the pane.
Her sun is the ceiling. His stars are the floor.
She bites her knuckles until he feels pain.
She knows his thoughts while he still has to guess.
He knows when she knows what he has to learn.
His favorite word is *now*. Her word is *yes*.
Apart, each is only radiant stone,
but one touch brings them to critical mass.
He likes to burn things and she likes to burn.

Say the sentence "It is hot in this room" and mean: "It is cold"

It is hot in this room. Outside, red snow
drifts against a birch's swollen, bone-white base,
ecdysiate tissue connected now
only by tendons to tibia, tarsus,
arthritic metatarsals of a one-
legged skeleton, its ramage arms raised
in the longing for flight of feathers in stone
or a show of strength or a posture of praise.
It is hot in this room. The windows sweat;
the knuckles of the birch tree wipe their brows.
A pack of snowflakes, frenzied from the heat,
circles the wind at the corner of the house,
dogs exhausting a prey too large to eat.
The orange eye in the ashes starts to drowse.

When the liberties are left unrestricted they collide

The way small birds collide with closed windows,
the way two planes collide in mid-air,
the way icicles in an uneven row
shaped like a scribbled musical score
impale the drift of two-day-old snow
beneath them when they fall from a gutter,
the way a fist batters an unshaven jaw
liberties collide with one another
and leave behind them holes or bruises,
greasy silhouettes or broken bones,
chalk outlines of contorted bodies,
craters, brushfires, footprints, lacerations,
skid-marks leading up to shattered glass,
or light, intense heat, and free electrons.

Both worlds are real, of course, and interact

In one the weight of water keeps the crust
from crumbling. The glaze on a T'ang vase,
concentrating color in the cracks, just
as barely supports its porcelain. Lace
is not more delicate, nor the dust
sun-chapped into scales on the surface
of the other, where nothing fails to taste
of salt and sun and some distant place.
That light when it changes media distorts
means that from the other world each looks less
like itself than like the one it orbits
so no one knows where we are in this
bright world where the last one standing eats
the black butterflies exhaled from the abyss.

Intercourse amounts to a hybridization of specialization

The man with the crooked dick writes his will.
The woman with one arm waves him goodbye.
What starts out *I love you* ends *go to hell;*
Do unto others, an eye for an eye.
He sneaks out the window, she flees through the door.
He meets someone with a skinnier ass.
She wants more children, he wants a fast car.
She meets someone with a vacation house.
It's hard to remember which happened first:
no talking, no fucking, no wrinkled shirts,
no touching in bed, no cooking breakfast.
It's hard to choose one from all the alerts:
no more shared showers, seeing whole newscasts
(no longer missing the weather and sports).

Let the stranger now enter the soul

No one awaits when she answers the door.
No one responds when she answers the phone.
A woman's face she has seen somewhere
watches, bodiless, from the reflection
behind her own reflection in the mirror
night makes of the stairwell window, but when
she turns she finds only the empty stair.
In some rooms, she has chills for no reason.
Soon enough she learned no one would listen,
soon enough, that no one would understand.
She learned to hold everything in, even
nights when the dog's whimper was the one sound,
when she watched, hugging herself in her nightgown,
the empty porch swing rock without wind.

No less than twenty-six distinct necronyms

Father dead, we will call her, or *Niece dead.*
Cousin in car crash. So many names fit.
Sister cut wrists, Brother shot in the head.
Grandfather wandered off, Great-uncle hit
by train while drunk. Aunt dead. Aunt dead. Aunt dead.
Brother stillborn. Uncle had heart attack.
Niece murdered. Great-grandmother died in bed.
Nephew dead. Sister drowned in frozen lake.
Sister burned in trailer home fire. Older
brother overdosed. Sister, crib death.
Cousin fell from third-floor window. Cancer
ate colons of two uncles, lungs of both
grandmothers. Cousin had kidney failure
after going blind. Mother died giving birth.

Hearing flute playing although there is no flute player

He finds in his desk the letter
she gave him no time to answer
or believe, the one he is sure
he burned long ago. *No other*
world, she says p.s., *can ever*
hold me. Love is never over.
On long-distance calls he can hear
her voice in those that interfere
in poor connections or bad weather,
soft whispers of a breathless lover.
One of her hairs falls from nowhere
onto his shirt, as if she were
alive still, teasing him, aware
even now of his ache to touch her.

Music can be heard in the distance

Music can be heard in the distance,
if the cicadas' chirring can count
or the crickets' crisp, spaced insistence,
distant only as in seldom found.
Farther, though, beyond any car engines,
past panicked tags on a scratching hound,
past the mother calling for Con-*stance*,
past the plane beginning to descend,
there timbres a music not music
so much as the sound of snow on snow
summing itself to a moon-white lake
at cloud-cold elevation, below
other stars, humming the curt lyric
a meteor lumines, da capo.

When I strike the match so close to the gasoline

I know what I'm doing when
I strike the match
so close to the gasoline.
And, when I touch
your hair, your earlobes, your chin,
what color each
gesture will be when it burns.
I know how much
heat it takes for human skin
to break into flame,
and what sort of combustion
I want, what time
I want it, in what conditions,
and with whom.

ORDERS OF MAGNITUDE

Here begins the work of darkness in which
I've been encrypted these ten pent terms past,
my tome of tombs, the lie in skull-script
I leave in lieu of a life. Here begins
my negative, in which corneas all
are black, pupils and irises all white,
in which you are darkness, damn you. Let this
be fair warning, let it loose a lesson,
but not pretend truth. Here starts the work of
darkness in whose delicious lap I lie.

•

I subscribe neither to species nor sex.
Weightless, I lean not into wind or wall.
I hear sniper fire in Sarajevo
but stay safe from clawing my shattered shin
to pull out the pain. I ride through riots
in L.A. but am not dragged from my rig
to read and reread iron. The short ride
from *Honey hand me my pants* to *I have
to do what's right for me* I know because
friends call when they arrive. These are their words.

•

Everything takes on a new appearance
after your daughter has drowned. Think yourself
into this: school trip to the lake, you're late
to her carpool, say *Hurry!* but forget
to kiss her goodbye, no one notices
when she goes under, a diver combing
for coins finds her face down on the bottom.
Everything takes on a greenish-brown tint.
Every step, your feet find mud and algae.
Water tests everything now, and all gold sinks.

•

Shocking disasters lie deeply hidden
in comforting numbers. Bodies surface
downstream, flesh pale as fish. Dogs sniff out their
scattered limbs. Boys find them under bridges.
Shocking lies hide deeply. Famine favors
foreigners. Humans die in comforting
numbers. A dog eating a corpse begins
with the brain. Promise. Disasters surface
downstream: scattered limbs, suffocated fish.
Hidden shocks favor humans. Breathe deeply.

　　　•

Water searching for itself under rocks.
Rocks rounded down by curious water.
Trout twinned with water, with stones streamed slick.
So many guilelessnesses sprung from such
a sire, a god by the name of chaos,
so many songs sung to the human eye.
First rocks become trout and trout become light,
then light becomes water and water song.
Last, the human eye can hear God wading
across trout-slick stones, searching for himself.

　　　•

Go and look behind the altar. My god,
my broken half-god, cowers there weeping.
Tears and drool mingle in his rheum-stained beard.
Tiny ash-fragile angels worship him,
singing a song of melting cellophane,
sizzle of ice crystals singed off a log,
snap of burning sap. Look behind my god;
look through him. Skin brittle as burned paper.
He weeps not for his own long withering
but for my short solo, sung sans seraph.

　　　•

It's not the satin-lined coffin I mind,
but the store-bought sympathy card before.
Not stopped heart, flat EEG, dry mirror,
but testicular cancer, breast cancer,
colon cancer, chemo weeks all baldness
and wretching, the incisions, excisions,
decisions, the futile hard-on that marks
the moment of death. Sponge baths, cold bedpans,
latex gloves. Not having to leave this world,
but having to bow so low to do it.

      •

The cat that killed the cardinal chick needs
the nourishment to care for its kittens.
Long live reproduction, long live hungry
mouths, the boy who beats up his brother for
the last ice cream bar, the brother who gets
beaten up but whom hunger educates.
Let there be ever more of us: eating
each other means we are not losing to
emphysema or meningitis. May
the parent birds live to lay next year's egg.

      •

The time of the earthquake. The character
of the crime. *You piece of shit.* Words to sing
on the way to school. Words to remember.
Words to live by. *You. piece. of. shit.* Help comes
after earthquakes and crimes. One day's whiskers.
One day's tears. One day's left-out, left-behind.
This will teach you to lie to me again.
In time for the earthquake. In time to sing.
You piece of shit. Sing the brutal, fetal
honesty of honest brutality.

      •

I used to canoe across cold tidal
marsh to the mouth of hell, warned well away
from nest stands tall as gallows by osprey's
spread wings. An osprey's one expression says
No forgiveness. An osprey's gaze insists
God sees us through hunters' eyes. The currents
here in strong tides will take you out to sea.
Gutted by gulls, crabshells litter the point.
I used to row right through the rushes past
ospreys to the mouth of hell. And go in.

    •

I first found blackberries more dangerous
than nipples, more pernicious to bared flesh
than hornets' nests, when a low cloud caught me
climbing Ragged before dawn. I wanted
to see sunrise from the summit, the long
spine of the other hills, a hawk circling
below me. I wanted to smell the coast,
take the next range's measure, but I saw
the cloud and I stopped for the blackberries
that stained me with their juice and my own blood.

    •

Spring sang saturated roses sinking
under superfluity, bent down by
embarrassing abundance, but summer
lurched in today like lightning, sudden heat
asserting its surmises: what was lost
found by the flash, fetched from sodden shadows.
Late but swarming like locusts, the extreme
temperature of transubstantiation
suffocates our bodies that beckoned it,
begging to become, impossibly, God.

    •

To prove God moves on the wings of the wind,
how many hawks watching from how many
road signs, fenceposts, treetops? How red their wings
when at rest, how white in flight? How many
mice must die, how elegantly, to feed
their wheeling? How many Canada geese
clattering from how many stubble fields,
their panicked rising from the horizon
thunderhead dark, need to settle onto
this frozen lake to show the angels fell?

    •

When angels fall in love, whole new hells form.
The explosion flashes across the sky.
In classrooms the wide universe over
children weep inconsolably, branded
by the flames, eyes shielded from the plunging
parabola of smoke. Rubble plummets
to the wave. After deaths that send out light
no bodies surface. The other angels
still mimic galaxies in clustered praise,
but their refrains ever after are lies.

    •

I set God free from the owl that waited
too late, spread wide wings too slowly. Next day
from the pronghorn that tried to stop but slid
across wet asphalt in front of my truck.
Now God speaks again, from the pendulum
tracing earth's arc in sand, from the rhythmic
rap-rapping of the roofer's air hammer,
pleated squeals of schoolgirls trampolining.
I set God free to speak to me again.
I no longer understand, but I hear.

    •

God's two wills, *Screen Door Banging in the Wind*
and *Melting Snow Sliding off a Windshield*,
will learn to hear each other's calls across
seasons lost to unlikeness. Got to kill.
Turn now: wind means more banging. No slow snow
sloping down will shield you. Wait for more heat.
God, you still mean screen door, T-shirt, low rent,
earn our roof the wrong way, sweat stains, sweet shame
the color of blood. I will get you back.
Got to know how. God, too, will learn to bow.

      •

I am accustomed to contests: my first
tug-of-war was to the death. Tightening
the nurse-noose around my neck, mother tried
at every contraction to strangle me.
I tried to eviscerate her with that
very vein, and did. So I'll die later,
more slowly, in the infernal method,
by corrosives: father's lifelong failure
to forgive, infrequent but vivid dreams,
distrust of songbirds' songs, sung in contest.

      •

The thought of death is my dancing partner,
a fine one. She laughs too much, but we whirl,
I a fallen leaf, she the wind. Stars swirl,
a mirrored ball, such fiery tesserae.
The thought of dancing with my fine partner
is death, but she won't let me sit. I've drunk
too much. She swirls like the night sky. Sweat beads
light her fine, fiery face. I've swirled too much.
She says she wants me. She's drunk. I'm dizzy.
The thought of dancing with my death is fine.

      •

Three hundred years leaves little legible.
The dates of mothers dead at twenty-five
beside their daughters dead at nine. Winged skulls,
winged cherubs, winged portraits. Nothing but blurs
in marble or sandstone, which last hardly
longer than we. Granite fractures and slate
segments. Stones sink and slant. Neither risen
nor fallen knew enough to name their new
condition something they will recognize
when next we call or next they need to know.

    •

Look at the person on your left. Now look
at the one on your right. This time next year
both will be gone. Or this time tomorrow.
History's pecker has eyes. History
can count higher than you, and hold its breath
longer. Look at the smile framed on your desk,
the ones in your wallet. History rolls
like the slow motion film of a fall. With
nothing to grasp, our arms describe perfect
circles; our arc to earth, history's grin.

    •

In a moment everything is altered.
The world spins from a thread tied to one leg
of a hovering sparrowhawk, whose wings
conduct the choir of invisible stars.
Field mice freeze in worship while cold stars sing.
At this altar, each moment has moment.
Here, now, the falcon is the one true god.
She names herself Lightness, names our world Weight.
Swings the pendulum, frays the thin thread, falls
one feather. This moment is everything.

    •

Trapped in the meshes of this neural net,
this translucent tissue, their tenuous
evanescences: voices, butterflies,
bells, taking shape as one body this gauze
knows by heart. And recites, neck to navel,
nipple to knee. Light shone through thought shows bells
and butterflies clinging, their bright talc wings
sand mandalas tapped out by bent Buddhists,
flour-fine voices of past lovers cooing
like doves huddled on a wire in the rain.

•

I love the world, as does any dancer,
with the tips of my toes. I love the world
more than I love my wife, for it contains
more crannies and crevasses, it tenders
more textures to my twenty digits' touch.
Lush grass underfoot after April rain,
small piles of petals fallen from roses,
sun-seared sidewalk in summer, sand, fresh-turned
garden dirt, and, yes, her hummocked ankle
rubbed by the ball of my foot as she sleeps.

•

My wife flames in all the colors of gems,
glows glossy as polished igneous rock,
flares like phosphorus. Her lips and hands melt
my misshapen face to pink lava flow.
My wife's fingers flash like the welder's flux,
her feet spark the same blue high C wheels sing
when subway cars scrape sharp turns. My wife burns
herself into me like specks of iron
ground in red showers from sawn steel. The scars
she leaves deform me but they make me hers.

•

I have seen her assume the forms of trees,
mountains, calling loons; seen her disappear
into a glacial lake when I canoe
too close; seen ospreys rise from her, and storms;
seen her green neck rise shining from the lake.
I have heard her speak the language of fire,
flowers, and sleepless nights, nights when the sky
explodes into fire and flowers, when sleep
flowers into the language of burning,
one of the languages I learned from her.

•

What every wife should know about her
husband's penis: it does not even need
itself. It prays alone to the Alone.
Like fire, this last limit of his body
ascends in pursuit of what it is not.
Think of it as his instead-of-a-soul,
possessed by lust for instead-of-the-truth,
which it seeks in the salt of origin,
finds altered there, your instead-of-nowhere,
fulfilling his need to become nothing.

•

By all accounts accountable to none,
fascinated with myself, with any
hollow place or prehensile appendage,
I am the leveraged buyout of reason,
the tail that wags the dog, the cat that ate
the coal-black canary, the kid who can't
count and won't learn, not now, the black sedan
passing slowly, twice, in front of your house,
I am the citizen penis, the boys
approaching you on a dark street, laughing.

•

Having fallen so far so suddenly
to so deep darkness, the first last darkness
and the only, only you can end so
long exile, so celestial distance.
So stepfather consoles stepdaughter. So
cold a hand, he claims, as mine could be drawn
only to so hot a flame as yours. We
both surrendered. I didn't know the moon
came in so many colors, or said no
as quietly and as often as snow.

                    •

Are love and rage one passion? Here, frozen
in the hell of violent sensations,
questions burn like ice. Is there a god? *No.*
Was there once a god? *No.* Will God crush you
as he crushed your father and your father's
father? *Yes.* With secret pleasure? *No, with
plainly visible pleasure. The pleasure
birds act out on berries, children on bugs,
bears on salmon, lovers on each other.*
Are love and rage the same? In me? *Hell. Yes.*

                    •

Sinister shade, source, soul, shared silhouette,
sun-severe singer of curses, singer
of tears, father, can't you see I'm burning?
Don't you see the fallen candle, the sheets
in flames, my singed arm, the others sleeping?
Don't you see the others sleep when you do?
Don't you see I can't? See, I had to die
before you would listen. I had to clutch
the kerosene for this protest, tug your
sleeve with the same hand soon to strike the match.

                    •

From frozen tarn to marmots' cries to moose
everything said *mountain mountain mountain*
in the sun-silvered morse of my own breath.
Everything said I'll breathe before my death
the very days he breathed before my birth.
Loud the sky sounds from inside. The sky shouts
the boy he played baseball with after work
plays ball with someone else's boy today.
No spent life wholly lost, no frost not now
another's cold breath. The clouds called me to climb.

                    •

Time is the way cold weather and darkness
expand into Mercator projection.
Time is how the organic resists soul.
Time is why the body misbehaves. Time
is the pattern printed on the bedsheets
and how as cotton thins its colors fade.
Time is a boy who can't name his sister
but who can identify prime numbers,
solve long division problems in his head,
and state square roots to seven decimals.

                    •

Hope names its own absence, a galaxy
older than this universe, *God* the death
of death, water that does not eat light, light
that does not drink water. That means *grief*
names gratitude. For the sound of aspens,
for the chimney's shadow across bright bricks,
for the color of clouds in evening light.
Gratitude that sometimes the body goes
first, that some lives leave a taste like honey
in the rock, some deaths bid the hungry eat.

                    •

I still cry in places, but not the ones
you would expect. Usually my knees.
Their long, muted wail trails a line of ash
in these bones it burrows through to my ears.
Less often in the muscles of my back.
Not that they feel your absence less, only
the dog team waits out the heaviest snows:
they pace and howl, but finally they sleep.
Seldom, thank god, in my forehead, which cries
silently, oblivious to the rain.

     •

Then, when facing the future resembled
staring west over a steering wheel at
I-80 leaving Lincoln, you could be
nothing but numb. But don't you feel grief *now*?
Now that happiness has reasserted
itself in her absence, now that molted
markings have been rendered in fresh feathers?
Isn't it now that sorrow shows itself
for what it is: the ease with which wounds heal,
and that in her absence you remain whole?

     •

Behind your kneecaps. In your left femur.
Radiating from your pelvis, lodging
between lumbar vertebrae. In your teeth.
You can feel grief even there, in your teeth.
It scalds your tongue and throat like hot coffee.
It spreads through you, confident as cancer.
Nothing is so delicious. Nothing feels
more like a bird trapped inside your body,
crashing into walls and windows over
and over while the cruel light pours in.

     •

Does this site-specific storm system make
me a woman, this ovarian cyst
swelling so close to my soul? Must I die
as a woman to have lived as one? Here,
take these feet of sewn seaweed, this brown mask
braided from corn husks. Bury them with me.
If earth wants herself back, I will oblige.
This core sample, one inch for each of my
forty-three years, shows the colors of soil
I've become. Earth is a woman I know.

     •

If I look down long enough my life looks
like the sky. Crows' tracks registered in mud
reiterate the flocks of geese that cross
my body twice a year crying *Die, die*
horizon to horizon. Looking up
I become the earth: prairies giving birth
to birds that rise in chorus, a single
vulnerability returned like breath.
We called our forgetting the land *flight*. Now
only our fall could recall it to us.

     •

When Thales learned to measure in his head
the surface of earth he made a ledger.
The annual Nile flood that gave us mud
gave us maps, calendars imposed on space,
the tablature of number's song. If light
does not seep through a surface, water will.
Burned skin rises, buried bones find the sea.
Pass through one portal into another.
Drive the square-mile county roads in Kansas.
Count the soft woven squares that conceal us.

     •

Once a couple of lovers. A couple
of cold friends now. How impotent the hand,
how infinitesimal the abyss
fingertip to fingertip when we stretch,
you prone across the ice, me the scared kid
who fell through. Close enough to have sparked once.
Close enough still to attract iron filings
formed after our former affinity.
Every couple repeats the history
of tangents that once touched but touch no more.

·

The thirty-third time I heard it, your name
became the blaze that blackened parched prairie,
the fire that opened cones under old growth.
Nothing nurtures like repetition,
or so exposes us as sagittal
sections arranged in rows. No thing repeats,
but all proportions do. Powers of ten,
atom to galaxy. You are to me
as fire to canvas, as tree ring to earth,
as number to a subjugated god.

·

So much for angles and fractions and maps.
It remains now to speak of curvature.
Ice-bent birch branch. Spruce soundboard. Marble hips.
What walks on Euclid in the morning, Gauss
at noon, and Marilyn in the evening?
Never smile at strangers. Don't accept gifts.
Don't carry someone else's bags on board.
A streetlamp given its halo by mist.
Light from one star bent around another,
masking planets only numbers can see.

·

Grant me a very crude notion of truth:
say six of the sages are guitar strings,
say the seventh files five long fingernails,
say Granados is God. Grant me that truth
mimics fog-muted church bells, soft rainfall,
thrush's song, that under the stars it sounds
like the stars, like the moon-silhouetted
nighthawks and swifts skittering for insects.
Reason resides in resonant rosewood.
Grant me that. Grant me that strings cannot lie.

        •

I confess I have failed you as the sun
in the far northern fall fails finally
and glows a slowly deeper, fainter blue
through leaning megaliths of quiet ice,
offering for months only auroras.
I confess I am wicked as winter
is dark, cruel as frostbite, still keep secrets
the way a snowscape hides a polar bear.
Gonechild long orphaned, I still have six sides,
and no one of me matches another.

        •

In the new world what flows off whale's flukes
before they sink in slow slow-mo like lives
that flaunt their long leaf-inevitable
leaving will be your song to sift, will sing
through you as thunder and rough light shout
when waves overwhelm precarious rocks.
There the stars I see through black trees will swarm
to your shoulder while you watch the old earth.
In it your life will glint silver as breath.
I owe you a world, and I plan to pay.

        •

I make it my principle to watch you
undress. When you bend for a sock, I count
your vertebrae. I know your underwear
from ten feet, I have pet names for each pair:
Lucky, Climber, Omigod. I make it
my principle to be first in bed, last
to close my eyes. I count your breaths. Some nights
I reach a thousand before I can sleep.
If I could die watching you, I would make
it my principle to shorten my life.

•

If bodies are clothes, they should be removed.
Sung, if they are songs. If cats, stroked and stroked.
But if bodies are bodies, already
they cling and purr and sing. Almost without
our help they come unbuttoned and drop down
to ankles that are nearly ours. Without
our hearing them or knowing where they were,
they rub against us, eyes closed, backs arched. When
bodies are bodies, they curl in our laps
and their quiet, half-growled *mmmm* is music.

•

Songs surround us, but we hardly hear them.
Jostling girls laugh in rapid Japanese.
The neighbor's sprinkler fortes for the part
of its arc that frets the climbing rose. Crows
bicker. One woman solicits her scales,
a cappella. Another sobs. Windchimes
domino the direction of each gust.
A broom rasps across warped, weathered porch boards.
I did it, Mama, a child says. Songs fall
on us as feathers fall on a river.

•

Centaurea cyanus, commonly
called cornflower, once bachelor's button,
croons blue in Finno-Ugric caroming
pine to pine, carols blue in Germanic
careening over the plains. Cornflower
can't be confined or claimed, knows no revenge,
only travel, only bloom, only blue.
No republic holds it, no soviet,
no reich. Blue speaks a universal tongue.
Indigenous to Europe. Escaped. Free.

    •

God being gone, love having left, our sole
remaining hope is to inflect complex
numbers. We know they follow daffodil
but anticipate iris and dogwood.
Early blossoms up, final flurries down
figure the square root of negative one.
Something other than integer squeezes
color from frost. Only complex numbers
can tell how far we need-based petals fall,
our very buds beginning our descent.

    •

Cat with no collar, spaniel at Sonic,
man sporting green suspenders on the plane.
The gods judge us by how we handle strays.
How many ticks can one coffee can hold?
Experiments in the ruins of math,
we run together like days, like numbers
for checkout boys who can't count back our change,
notes for untrained fingers on untuned strings.
One-and two-and three-and . . . More grounds slurry
the mug than days remain in our blurred lives.

    •

Let me start over. Not so I can speak
clearly, but so I can mimic the gods.
When they command the wind the wind obeys
its own will. I understand the devil's
one melodious truth but not the gods'
polyphonic paradox. Not so I
can say something else, but so I can mean
more by the same thing, more than I meant then,
more than I can know I mean now. More than
the gods, who understand all but themselves.

•

The rules: Make your own lane. Make eye contact
only with equals. Yield to oncoming
traffic. Walk faster than any footsteps
following you. If the Manual wreaks
havoc in the bed, throw it out. Alone
means lost, as does dark. Looking out, not up,
doubles the rent. God sits on the left side
of the plane flying in, and so should you.
Speak seldom, and in prosthetic language.
This skyline alone remains of the soul.

•

Here where trees grow up to the street, we need
every possible manner of prayer:
stout toddler stopped at the top of the slide,
open guitar case, extra coin offered
the meter. Why-not glance through the peephole,
window box profligate with white pansies.
We stay on our knees and no longer speak.
We need bike helmet, shoulder belt, sunscreen,
used paperback on the subway. We pray
with sunglasses, housesitters, mace. Hear us.

•

Airfield first, harbor later. My discharge,
due the next day, was delayed by a month,
then brought at last by mortar shell. Certain
Japanese magicians, known to the west
now as legend, could make fall back to earth
alive and restored to wholeness a child
they had cut to pieces. The magician
I watched passed close enough, strafing the dorm
where I stood watch, for me to see his eyes.
I have seen in this life no child made whole.

     •

Liters in hand, wind-bent eyot lives leave
before fish-filled styrofoam flats replace
the milk in the mailboat's hold. Not a tree
limns this archipelago. Human blood,
salty as this sea, here flows just as cold.
Here, what is not rock or water is wind.
Death is wind, and regret, and loneliness.
No concession, no cure. No fish, no milk.
Brown-and-white hulls rock in the mailboat's wake.
On the dock stands a blond girl named Regret.

     •

She was wild veronica until she
discovered the lure of iris and rose
and lily-of-the-valley. Any grave
would want to wear her, festooned with her friends.
As a child veronica discovered
herself stemming in curls, swirled like a cape,
unfolding holding her friends' fern-frond hands.
Before she felt the lure of shady beds
loose with cool humus, mild veronica
grew grave. Until she discovered herself.

     •

Leave the package at the door. I will be
tied up. I suck at the Great Mother's breasts,
tipple Tetons, enjoy her Jane Mansfields.
If I ask nicely, she shows me a mean
sunset. I ask nicely. I fondle her
flora and fauna for as long as she
lets me. She lets me as long as I want.
Goddess, she's good, Grand Canyon to K-2.
She nudges me to nibble everything
edible, and everything of her is.

·

A master plaster caster I know made
molds of both his pricks. Prize peckers, I'm told
by one who knows. Well hung, the molds serve her
as tintinnabula, but torment him.
It's nearly impossible to appease
two penises at once. I try to please
both of mine. Tried. I tried taking tinfoil
casts to compare, so they could see themselves
as others do. Other. Significant.
Who flies just fine without my wings or bells.

·

I imagine whole *species* multiplied
by my sense organ, Sam. Whole worlds, if Sam
had his way. Sam's hardly a sensible
organ. Seldom does Sam listen to me,
though he holds my attention. Sam's sixth sense
pricks my other five. Sam brags a fetish
for certain shapes and colors, certain smells,
certain ways of moving and forms of speech.
Sam flaunts as many fetishes as I.
I make Sam obey. He makes himself heard.

·

Hell's teeth, you're right. We should have. Hell's mouthwash.
By your wife's plump farts and infrequent lusts,
by my half-husband's half-hearted humping,
you're right. Hell's cold sores. Hell's discolored tongue.
If only to prove our first passions wrong,
to fail where we could fail fully and well
instead of where we had failed already,
we should have. By her dimpled thighs and his
pimpled ass and our poor judgment, you're right.
Hell's breath. Hell's hot, wholly intent kisses.

      •

Do you rejoice at your sister's pleasure,
really? Are you truly happy for her
when she asserts herself so well she drops
all difference between man and woman,
finger and tongue, dick and machine? Do you
want to hug her because she feels she is
the ocean, because her saltenness flows
without her will, because she bites her lip
so hard it bleeds? Do you worship with her
lover at All Holes Church? Do you believe?

      •

Men kneel when she offers the fruits of her
experience: both breasts, all four nipples.
All she knows shows itself in infrared,
including the specters surrounding her,
not dead enough to be happy, barely
alive enough to be free. Tenebrous,
half in hell, fully in love with licking,
too far from her lignite to flame. Men kneel
when they see so many outlines to trace.
They fade from one earth into her other.

      •

Lord let my lover be no less laissez
than she is fair. Engender her, Jesus,
so she wants out of her jeans as often
as I want in them, make her generous
as algebra, who gives more than is asked
of her, who surprises petitioners
with unexpected solutions to cold
nights and thunderstorms, knows y and y naught,
likes the spot x marks (lingers over it),
kneads perfect numbers from bellies and knees.

•

I would take my lovers, had I any,
to my studio, had I one, to drink
Jack Daniel's or Wild Turkey, whichever
looked more like that day's sun, if the sun shone,
and remind them of parts of themselves they
had thought forgotten, if I could not work,
or because I cannot and no longer
want to, since the body's judgment betters
the mind's and it takes lovers to forget
suns, and suns whiskey, and whiskey myself.

•

Men are not required to collaborate
in dreams. A clone in mine begged to borrow
my briefs. Marriage, men, grows flowers and heat,
glowers, not an institution profused
for a few. Here the masses burrow in
briefly, to nibble on flowers and hide
from the heat. When she wakes to a burro
in my underwear, will she be required
to love that ass no less than she loves mine?
Marriage makes mean dreams. Men are not required.

•

A black face surrounded by a bright light.
A dress in sea-turtle green in the place
her scarlet bodice had been. Her double,
the figure of her well-favored figure,
in complementary colors, as if
she had not turned away. Always
I watched from some distance, always she stood
in half shadow. Not quite her, not quite here,
she floats between the white wall and my mind,
there where she is not, her black hair white hot.

     •

How could I taste her lips and not my own?
How could I feel her thigh around my thigh
but not mine around hers? How could I smell
her hair but not my nose, feel her rough felt
and inferno but not feel my finger,
and taste the sweet dew morning envies her
but not taste my own tongue? How disappear
into her so wholly without naming
the cries my very spine hears as only
from her, without feeling my breathing stop?

     •

A man holds out his hands who wants to know.
How to sate her hungers, and how his own.
Which bulbs to plant in fall, which to dig up.
How to tell the children their dog has died.
Whether to bury it there in the yard.
How to fetch orgasm with no later
ill effects. Whether he would feel better,
forgiven one of the twelve steps and one
commandment. Why he dreams so often now
of mountains, but so seldom of the sea.

     •

He fondles women, but does not really
rape them. Our irises grew late this spring;
the redbud barely bloomed. Any breeze helps
a day this damn hot. I did see someone
suspicious on the street today. I hope
hummingbirds will find our cannas this year.
When she had not returned half a life late,
I went out searching. Songs are hard enough;
maybe prose is impossible. How can
lace this thin let in so little sunlight?

     •

Timid flakes like birds' ghosts peck the window,
wanting in. Stay and starve, migrate and die.
What song gets sung but *Feed me*? Maple leaves
lilt to oblivion. In the garden
one last rosebud opens to this first snow.
Birds' ghosts feed the division of labor
in the sexual act. Snowflakes make like
maple leaves: migrate and die. When the earth
sings *Feed me*, we join the round. One rosebud
hungers for snow. One leaf labors to earth.

     •

No red so gold, no orange so bloody,
no roan so brashly ablaze as what flocked
for fifty falls to one now-felled maple.
Those colors' migration from a solstice
apprenticed to puffins' beaks, wildflowers,
and the midnight sun ended one autumn
at a building not their tree. One autumn
I will build a home for homeless colors.
It will look like the lives that once bore them,
and sound like a grosbeak in the first snow.

     •

Call the cliff-face reason while the clips hold,
the ice-sheet truth till it cracks. Call the wind
revelation, the rapids melody.
Still the wisest god could compose no song
more canorous than tunes our fool tongues croon
while we drown, refrains our fingers figure
while we fall. Forgive my frequent missives,
friend, but each inflection may be final,
so I sing not to the infinite but
to you whose fated failure matches mine.

            •

After October snow overburdens
the trees and bends their branches to the ground
or the breaking point, whichever comes first.
After stars replace the branches' neck-sharp
snapping with their imitation of grace.
Save God for later. After the same snow
that pulled down power lines melts into flood
and spills across thresholds into dark rooms.
After the next front affords frost that blasts
the rose and prints white fossil ferns on panes.

            •

Daguerreotype muffled under silver
velvet. Gilt majuscules suffocating
in incunabula. I seldom hear
angels call from the clouds, though
the pawn-sized posturing of pennyworths
I know says I should. The gods gave me up
long ago, so I lift thick flock fabric
from tintypes in dim rooms, rub my fingers
down embossed spines, and pray to dead angels
who made their revelations, given none.

            •

My first cup of conviction made me retch.
My last cup of courage taught me to count.
The truths numbers tell best end at zero,
though so do their lies. Water knows the one
direction it needs. Light, how to stay warm.
In whose arms, at whose hands, on whose pillow.
At the end of my row give me water
and light and numbers that end in zero,
a name for the color clouds will be just
when I look up, but never quite again.

                    •

A little oatmeal lotion to relieve
the itch, a little morphine for the pain.
Toxins told her all the news she needed.
No more dialysis, she said one day,
adding *no more rain* to the *no more snow*
she did not choose. Her daughters bathed her, one
her legs, one her face, one their origin.
She weary, sister. Doan git so wary.
Eyes open in her final sleep, she said
I see God! What does he say? *Nothing yet.*

                    •

God he spoke and then the chariot stop.
Never mind she was forty-six and he
was fifty-two. The eighteen-wheeler spoke.
Never mind this was her first best marriage
and she was a virgin. Never mind they
had just left the church. The chariot stop.
Never mind it was dragged a quarter mile.
The sparks they sang. The driver he saw God
bearing down, but saw one cut-short breath late.
God! he spoke. But then the chariot stop.

                    •

Only after drifts covered my cold car
did I know I would die there. Snow stores light.
Even under a twelve-foot drift, at night,
in a storm, after frostbite has greeted
your ankles, snow *glows*. Dimly, but it glows,
loaded with bright angels that floated down,
jellyfish adrift in a cold black sea.
I gave in to sleep, already chalk, white
under layers of lives that will rise up
in ten million years to glint in the sun.

     •

Señoritas mummied in Juarez sun,
pants around their ankles, beetle holes bored
in black cheeks, blank eyes. Pakistani boys
bent over looms. Did I fail to mention
the price of light? What looks like luxury
is. We, God's compound eye, witness the world,
his body, burned by the halogen bulb.
Fire in the east, fire in the west. Plenty
to trust the truth, plenty to deny it,
none but Lucifer left to know better.

     •

The hawk enfolded in the fist fights song
by crying warning. Six white hares huddle
in the held breath. The body's borrowed speech
is our only speech, its hush all we know
of silence. Even when we overhear
the rain, we need translation into touch.
Nothing speaks like bone stridulating bone.
Nothing ciphers like fingertip to wrist,
the clicks and hums of whale calling to whale
in language older than the sea is vast.

     •

Next to the only room left in our world
(a screened porch with space for the two of us,
our rocking chairs, and as end tables slabs
of rough-cut elm balanced on old cream cans)
I've planted angels, wild perennials
that call across mountains and parallels
to hummingbirds and through old growth to bees.
He and I live a pestilence and die
a meteor but my sweet profligate
cherubs scent days too furious, too few.

                    •

How do you like paradise so far? Stay.
All charm burns off like morning rain. Crabs clean
these rocks by hand. You'll yet regret feelings
so exquisite. Earth screamed our birth with fire:
the end will come when the sea loses count.
One god named the old island, another
will name the new. Teach me to lay my eggs
in sand, I'll teach you to breathe in the sea.
Watch for the silhouetted shearwater
at sunset zipping the horizon closed.

                    •

Rocks risen from rocks, rounded by roiling.
Clattering leaves atop coconut palms.
Clouds colored by contact: sea-dark below,
sun-bright above. For everything you know
but will not tell, something else surrounds you
without letting on. Smaller than nipples,
a million snails climbing the wet seawall.
Their ancestors disguised as sand teaching
crabs color, their sisters trapped in tidepools.
The soft, soft song of the susurrate surf.

                    •

What you call courage floats in the cold sea
longer than we do who shiver, then sink
out of sight of the sun. What you call love
I carved into a birch box I set out
each night with food for the new ghost, the one
who calls you Courage and names me Nothing,
though my face is his. Who will not set foot
on the porch if I am watching but floats
in the dark night longer than it takes me
to see my own face in yours while you sleep.

      •

Soften the mountain for centuries, then
swallow the city in minutes. Ships sink
near shore. The sea is the richest nation
after the soil. Two coins in every grave,
no eyes. The medulla oblongata
savors lovely and serious objects.
Swallow the ant in seconds, but save it
for centuries. Bury sons in the sea,
daughters in soil. Two pennies for your thoughts.
We must be safe out here, so far from shore.

      •

The negation of a relation is
a relation. Our negation I name
Nereus for the father I am not,
no matter our daughters' needs, no matter
my own. Nereus names how transient I
stay in their element, they in mine, how
unlike their water is my air. When you
negated me, my relation to them
turned orphan to orphan, but Nereus
none of us can negate, no matter what.

      •

I name myself Rosalind whenever
he beats me, because so little blood needs
emphasis, some red to balance the blue
of bruises that darken me as dampness
darkens dishrags. Because the bruises bloom
the way buds bloom: delicately, briefly.
To understand my mind, you would need to
understand my body the way he does,
as a sea turtle understands the earth
and tries to cry out to it but cannot.

•

An accurate self-portrait would not look
like me. Black bile and spit in a small vial—
there. Truth is hard to swallow. Pubic hair
bound in a bow. Shall I enumerate
my humors? Blood, bile, choler, come. Come, come:
how many more lies must I try, how much
closer must I stand before you see me?
I thought of eating a gun, but this death
seemed more revealing. My life. I call it
Self-Portrait in Shit and Underarm Hair.

•

My friends glimpse ghosts in stairwells and hear them
padding past office doors at night. My friends
wear gold rings given them by aliens.
They see Elvis. They talk to God. Why not,
when I have never doubted you loved me?
Why do we *believe* anything at all?
Where might I still hide the gold ring the sun
sold me? Why does your ghost take off its shoes
at my office door? Why will it not speak
in any voice except the voice of God?

•

Flutes, bells, human voices. Spring. Lawnmower
in thick grass, almost stopped, catching its breath.
The grating of a plumber's snake scraped up
and down the neighbor's gutters. Bells, voices,
calls of cardinals, weed trimmer whining
through wet grass, a dog jogging by, panting
with its master, the reeling of its leash
when it stops. I don't believe in gods, but
I believe in signs. The clack of roller-
blades across sidewalk cracks. Flutes. Oh, and bells.

                    •

Voices of geese crossing yellow night sky.
If it meant something other than itself
their song would sound less like God. If they meant
anything less than God, geese would not sing.
Over me music, under me water.
One family portrait per funeral.
Each year the geese name one more missing face.
Each season the hazed light that hides their flight
mutes their song. And the mist that soaks sidewalks
and stains roofs glints on cars under streetlights.

                    •

We have come in your dreams, a hundred eyes
atop the fence then moving toward you
through the dark yard like approaching planets,
to fulfill your own predictions. We've come
to say our names, to show how far they are
from yours. To leave urgent, inscrutable
messages, on which your life and the lives
of your children depend, to satisfy
an appetite you have misnamed *spirit*,
our name for which you cannot understand.

                    •

In case of police, I keep at all times
an emergency packet: a toothbrush,
toothpaste, razor, comb, soap, some underwear,
a good book, pen and paper, one leaf, an etui
with one relic, a lock of my wife's hair.
In case of the gods, I carry with me
the Estonian word that names winter,
a tune Brouwer calls "Berceuse," the six months
Alma Ettie saved for her daughter's trike,
the smell of lilac and mint after rain.

      •

My joints make noises when I kneel beside
the flowers. Nowadays my joints demand
always to be heard. I need a stick's help
to stand back up. I teeter between rows
of tomatoes, where soon a fall will break
a hip. My fingers no longer straighten,
nor does my back. I ask not to transcend
this body but to reclaim it. Not that
my husband's mind be right again, but that
he stop crying. I see nothing, clearly.

      •

Friends feel pain not at corresponding spots
but in the *same* place. Winter always feels
unusually cold here where its rules
demand exceptionally long darkness.
Friends feel rain despite the demands of snow.
Friends feel pain wherever time mislays it,
in an office savaged by Soviet
soldiers, in a sister's lost words, or propped
against the joy I feel when suddenly
I understand how to translate your life.

      •

At sea level earth still thinks it can rise,
the lungs still eat solid food. Desyatins
dense with dust, limestone-grained grasses lining
gravel roads, and serried smog-shrouded squares
sediment. See the stars or breathe. Hm. No
simple choice. I recommend burning legs,
a face blue as night. I recommend height.
Whatever else I do, I'll offer you
a mountain where only eyes can inhale,
where everything is ice or light. Or both.

                •

A yellow square revealed by scratching off
a black wash, the neighbor's kitchen window
frames an eggshell blue vase and her housecoat
the color of clover. A violent violet
sprayed across the sky presages thunder.
Through strict obedience to light, color
claims quite considerable liberty:
next day the same blue will spread horizon
to horizon the fragrance Ariel
inhaled in the new and limitless world.

                •

Cormorant perched atop a rocking mast.
Gull wheeling, then plunging into the sea.
Puffin staring across waves, a widow.
I speak here of angels, but I mean men.
Puffin flapping faster than angels' words.
Gull in wind flying backward, a devil.
Cormorant rocking, spread wings praising light.
Here, waves speak to men often of angels.
Widowed angels speak seldom of the sea.
Men tied to masts hear angels in the wind.

                •

The god of mathematics must have felt
this frustration when he fractaled feathers
enough for the first flight, then watched from earth.
I've serried syllables as I'm able,
numbered all I know and then some, but still
late snow blackens these bare branches as it
melts itself to mud, still skeletal dogs
stare from roadsides, already my digits
subtract my done days arthritically,
count this I've said against what I should say.

THISTLE, CLOVER, RAPE

Riga

Stones' scars never heal.

Souls fall like leaves from a linden. Souls mimic cottonwood seeds in the breeze.

Birds part for the passing of purpose.

In a world so badly blurred, who would not laugh at such scattering?

Suffering passes hand to hand and kiss to kiss.

Notes from phone calls to parliament pattern a woman's dress.

He praises most who sees tragedy first.

Five-year-old hands, fifty-year-old eyes. Small countries, paired histories.

One grandfather god starved in the gulags, one cello case hungers for change.

Stones sing second what we sing first.

Kaunas

Bend at the waist in the sun, at the knees under a roof.

Crucifixes, amber rosaries, Disney sunglasses.

Candlelight creates the face.
Flame must be flown toward.
What attracts angels consumes.

Crosses need no seeds to grow.

Count your paces across the square, or someone else will.

Bodies stand briefly, but sag back to the earth.

Here is how high the water rose last time we died.

Vilnius

The drunken man's staggering makes the sober men lurch.
Even with an arm around its waist, this world cannot stand.

Seven stars, seven flowers: the years to come, holding hands.

Cathedral of the Black Madonna.
Cathedral of the Crowded Bus.
Cathedral of Water Heated on the Stove.

Hold heaven in your hand, but leave it here.

Children fallen, mothers risen. Saints nesting in the trees.

Of course beauty is in another tongue. *Of course* you cannot understand.

Tallinn

Its inscription goes, but the sculpture stays.

Who knows no ceiling sees the sky.

Women on one side, men on the other, God in the middle.

Three steps into the earth: invitation to the spirits, head start for us.

Climb the hill to praise the sea.

Hiiumaa

Wait long enough, and even stones wash ashore.

What might have fallen from the sky did.

Some precincts suffer occupation only by their own.

A flower in my stead, a tree in yours.

Tartu

Confinement erases what liberty writes.

Here my father's fall broke my mother's ribs.

What separates us flows to the sea.

Broken through into this world, the next.
Side by side, staring across the river.

On a bright morning after long sleep, one person's hand on another's.

St. Petersburg

Three winters' seige starves a city to sawdust, seventy starves it to ash.

Citadels guard against the growls of prowling wolves, the gaze of a grazing doe.

Thin soup, thick bread.

Floating cities float on skeletons.

When cobblestones break falls, they break bones.
The backs that broke cobblestones, cobblestones broke.

Friendship sings with frenzied hands its inaudible, inscrutable song.

Light that leaves for a month returns for a day.

A sickle can be found for any harvest.

Four silent bells on the riverbank, four fish sing to the sea.

Buried lies rise as trees. Buried hope becomes the very earth.

More bodies, faster.

Mosquitoes' wings drown your soundest sleep.
What can enter your room at night enters your dreams.

A thin slit of light, a pair of eyes. Another hour.

Palace made to remain empty, tenement made to stay full.

Wary eyes, small room, locked door.

A death that cannot swim will fly.
Bodies sometimes swim. Souls always sink.

Stagnant waist-high water, waving waist-high weeds.

Lupine, thistle, clover, rape.

Even God falls into disrepair.

Moscow

Truth grins. Its loaded gun follows you across the cobbled square.

Water burns, water glows, water assumes all the forms of flame.

Sounds in the stairwell pad doors, transform flats into cells.

Caged beasts pacing collide at night.

Suffocating canaries, unclean cats.

Richest renewable resource: rust. Cash crops: crumbled concrete, broken glass.

Prudent savers of our currency, the lie, grow deaf within months.

At the current exchange rate, we cannot print bills in high enough denominations.

For every toast, a single swallow. Name a joy, drink a sorrow.

Contorted sleep on the subway. Sleep on the sidewalk. Sleep in the snow.

What cannot be cleaned will be painted over.
What cannot be painted will be burned.
What cannot burn cannot burn.

Lies in the water, lies in the air, lies in the crumbling walls.

We will hold your passport for the duration of your visit.
You must carry your passport with you at all times.

Eyes learn blindness.

The bus might not start. The train might not stop.

Because train tracks and needle tracks occur together.
Because the platform is crowded. Because she will not feel your feet.

A single scarf sweeps a brown line against a steady stream of shoes.
One bundle of twigs a broom. Two more, hands.

Clouds can carve their initials into lungs or sear them into stone.

You cannot understand. You are not dead like me.

Novosibirsk

So it would cease to flow, we named it the sea.

My voice among these trees sounds like shame.

Flowers under such a canopy create their own light.

Plastic-sheeted patios on prefab mausoleums.
Birdhouses for our timid, seed-eating souls.
Rusted vents for markers, root cellars for graves.

One bag of potatoes as ballast to balance another.

Leaning on its handlebars, a man pushes his bike up the path to Russia.

Scars connect Irkutsk to Moscow across a birthmark broad as the taiga.

Music fills falling warehouses, but must ply tins of caviar to leave.

Stack bricks high so windows stay above snow.

In the taiga's short spring, concrete composts in cold mud.

Steel rusts the color of the copper beech's bark.

More die of hunger in the bright weather before crops than starve in snow.

Who will give us a will of our own?

I am smoke in your face, fifteen, eyes already currency-hard.
You have what I need. I am what you want.

The God of Restlessness

These files in longhand litter . lies I tell myself
over shoulderblades . whose outlines I never traced
in eyes that took brown briefly . eyes that grazed mine green
then took back their grant .

. I arrange them by last name
made up when I can't recall . exchanged when I can

.

each scrap hoards stories . sandals and a summer dress
kneeling to weed a garden . the day after rain
standing to watch hummingbirds . suckle at cannas
holding to her chest . a sweating glass of iced tea
or the crying one . molting in a gazebo
talking to herself . her knees tucked under her chin
under indecisive clouds . urgent of iris

.

.

wind testing the house . threatens a storm that won't come
unless the threat *is* the storm . lightning highlighting
the horizon's hills .

. in calmer weather I leave
food for hummingbirds . food for titmice and finches
even for deer and raccoons . food for the elders
who never return . food for my unborn children
who refuse to eat . having no song to exchange

.

.

wall clinging to the burren . flat stone on flat stone
enclosing nothing . but measuring salt-mewed mist
scribbled signature . half-sister to the river
bright orange range fire . rewriting the horizon
yellow bales of hay . scattered across a green field

graying rows of fenceposts . warping loose their nails
knothole in one board . robin cocked on another

.

the elders still write . or rather what they wrote once
remains legible . two-hundred eighth-note blackbirds
inscribe a phone line . icicles mark a gutter
how long ago did they die . who remembers them
what can remembering mean . but to read their hand

.

it began in a body . that first character
one soot-stained index finger . swiped across elkhide
hand holding a bone . idly burrowing in dirt
fist furying flint . forth and back across sandstone
meditative tap and swirl . of bare feet in dust
one body beyond itself . branding another
spoke to bodies yet unborn . and now ours attend

.

as termites winnow timber . patiently to dust
as long rains incise hillsides . as wind sculpts sandstone
you my hallowed hollowed me .

. you might have saved me
if love belonged underground . attending echoes
of occasional droplets . dying in its rooms

.

.

elm grown wide as ice grows tall . solving for stone rows
another neighbor buried . in a paltry plot
shade seldom visits .

. in fulfillment of our grief
this rare endangered beauty . when we sought it least
one inevitable loss . praising another

.

.

was the missing child . abducted from her parents
or taken by them .

   . they pause before answering
no longer certain themselves . whatever they know
they know not to tell .

   . who leaves doors unlocked these days
even when they're home . wouldn't the baby have cried
and why did the dog not bark .

   . whatever they say
no one will believe . not sad enough or too sad

   .

so what if you rise early . and sing the loudest
lives stand headstone high . and the masters mostly lied
a hundred gilded haloes . feign beatitude
per Vermeer visage . lit divinely from within
I believed in souls . till mine grew wings and I fell

   .

summer of mud-covered boots . and mud-stiffened gloves
summer of singing off-key . of afternoon rain
summer of strangers . of someone else's small town
someone else's cars . cruising someone else's streets
playing someone else's songs . summer of paid cash
when the whistle wept . summer of all the old hymns
stop making sense when . even the devil has died

   .

summer of misreading rain . mishearing Spanish
summer of quicksand . fist-sized potatoes tumbling
to conveyer belts . summer her eyes matched the sky
blue for blue and deep for deep . empty for empty
I regret nothing . ask for nothing *am* nothing

   .

   .

before he started . hitting me I knew he would
her hands had started shaking . before she called me
by my brother's name .

. I knew when I topped the hill
first his fever spiked . the delirium followed
just because I knew . doesn't mean I tried to stop

.

suspended between . impression and idea
between crescendo . curtain and category
between cardinal . cracking seeds at the feeder
and cat crouched under porch steps . flicking her long tail
between cresting one last rise . and seeing the cars
crumpled and steaming . strewn across the snowy road
the first chemotherapy . and the futile next

.

between architectonic . and intuition
a voice listens for itself . but hears rain instead
hears the deer tearing . at undergrowth raise its head
pause and then bound out of sight . hears a last hoot fall
sees the owl's silhouette rise . from a bare oak branch

.

.

I lost count soon at seven . the drops fell so fast
seeing no shelter . she shed her soaked shoes and laughed
she shone shingle-bright . wet with light storm clouds restored
she shone like damp dogwood bark . dark with the rainlight
dark with duration . sustaining fugitive white

.

leaves float past motionless trout . watching for insects
one crow flies sideways . one fights a branch for balance
a thirsty collie kisses . its reflected twin
and in the garden . god's familiar shuffle shifts

leaves still fire-colored . bird-life long after falling
in last light from first sundown . of this last season
god's steps stop god's bird-heads turn . when I call her name
.

.

at any distance . in any color in some
new space-time continuum . better after death
quod est absurdum . with my tongue cut out because
you were there because . waxwings no longer pass through
so berries fall to the walk . wasted like seedlings
sprouting in gutters .

. for the very reason rain
would give if you could ask it . if it would answer

things fall she said nestling birds . leaves meteorites
facial features of lost friends . and dead relatives
chunks of bricks from unstable . chimneys angry words
debris from exploded planes . seeds for next summer
rocks childhood lessons rain snow . years from our one life
.

.

in a darkened room . the wick of a snuffed candle
resists expiration . its red-flicker tip rose-hot
its smoke a soul substitute . rises up swiftly
embodies the life . whose light makes it visible
and the death whose imminence . its faintness foretells
.

.

make mine that moment between . after the black wall
of nine-mile-high nimbus clouds . blocks the western sun
but before the storm attacks .

. after softer rain
starts darkening grass . but before its stain obscures

the dry shade-circle . protected by the maple
brighter for once than the rest .

. the moment Mozart
feels like it might shatter just . before the cadence

.

grant me the interstitial . indian paintbrush
rooted between rocks . colon setting ratio
my left hand between . your head and the pillowcase
you my enemy-lover . adversary-god
mantra-curse compass-polestar . lightning-rod-lean-to

.

.

it happened when I started . singing hope to sleep
the sycamore wants inside . scrapes siding and screens
afraid of the wind .

. Thirst wins over wariness

at the waterhole all bow .

. I have seen rainfall
in brightest sunlight . but not snowfall under stars

.

something listening . at the bottom of the stairs
something singing in the woods . just behind the house
something crouched in the bushes .

. if I were a bird
I would be an owl . able to fly silently
eyes the size of orange moons .

. if not I would sway
between trees and hypnotize . dew into spirals
I can name what I long for . but never aloud

.

which is smaller what was left . when you spit me out
or what I was before you .

. *of course* my vision

of the world is dark   .

          .   the plum tree blossomed too soon

and the blundering robins   .   built their nest too low

I was guilty of love once   .   but never again

          .

          .

the same head-high mud   .   that hallows water's passage

as flood across a first floor   .   threatens its return

measure and memory merge   .   into prophecy

and prophecy stains   .   stains will rot removed or left

water swift or slow   .   maps its every movement

          .

grass flow-combed across sloped yards   .   after a downpour

cracked sagging asphalt   .   worms dotting darkened driveways

blossoms battered from branches   .   onto sated grass

leaves soaked back to soil   .   canyons fossil trilobites

rock strata smooth stones   .

          .   after storms sweet ozone smell

red horizon that haloes   .   this ancient sea floor

twin salt tracks tears trace   .   down the contours of your face

          .

          .

thrown from the convertible   .   into new seasons

of parkinsoned syllables   .   scars like wildflowers

echoes in the room   .   that memories once furnished

seizures nightmares withered legs   .   and three friends fewer

the one who survived   .   had to be told who she was

and how she had been reborn   .   a less pretty girl

confined by squeaking white shoes   .   and wilting bouquets

          .

even storms give more warning   .   a darkening sky

and three full seconds   .   from first distant flash to sound

instead of the sudden slip   .   into fishtailing

the girls' screams their car . willful like a boy in love
choosing its own course . head-on into a mail truck
.
.
they stayed always chapped her hands . just like the woman's
who inhabited my dreams . it was how I knew
her hair the next day . copied the dream-woman's hair
from the night before .
. the dream-woman drew me down
in the barn behind a house . she loved as a girl
but I never saw .
. an owl perched in the rafters
watched us with her weightless eyes . it was how I knew

evidence flattens .
. a brittle browning flower
shadows its matching bruises . on facing pages
to say someone young . loved me once almost enough
black and white the soldier smiles . who killed my mother
months before my birth . who looks exactly like me
.
I try to forget my dreams . but still they recur
a woman inhabits them . the owl in the barn
anything I need to know . she says with her eyes
we wait together . for a fire to burn the barn
so I can see it . shining in her weightless eyes
her hands stay chapped all the time .
. whatever I know
falls through the visions she gives . that I don't believe
.
.
god of brief beauty . show me crocus blooms in snow
god of rotten two-by-fours . and *don't tell me no*

god of detonation sites   .   and training centers
god of the voice expanding   .   in the cathedral
god of restlessness   .   carry my words on your back

    .

god of flamed maple   .   and sixth string tuned down to D
god of hot springs and sinkholes   .   save me from my sight
god of spent casings   .   and constructive engagement
god of arthritic knuckles   .   elm blight elastic
god of mudslide and fever   .   unrequited love
god of listen in   .   and can't shit now without help
god of *no not me*   .   dry me from the outside in

    .

god of pierced nipple   .   and golden eagle tattoo
god of trilobite tapeworm   .   archeopteryx
truth god save me from   .   happily ever after
god of go-between   .   and lift me from the wheelchair
while the others cry for food   .   teach me flight and song

    .

god of tablets fat crayons   .   and dimpled knuckles
god of left beside the road   .

    .   god of bad grammar
god of shifting foundations   .   speak through cracked sheet rock
god of extra toes   .

    .   god of *anything but that*
let me hear cold branches creak   .   hear snow fall on snow

    .

god of lost in the blizzard   .   not found till spring thaw
god of couldn't sleep   .   truant god burn-unit god
give me if not her movement   .   the dancer's posture
give me what she thinks   .   suspended there in mid-air
for that one moment   .   make me her understanding
let my will outlast   .   what it cannot overcome
with each incision take back   .   some part of yourself

    .

    .

pair of house finches . nesting in the christmas wreath
neglected on the front door . field mice in the shed
the wait for seedlings .

. laughing women walking past
fresh cedar mulch outscenting . iris and roses
two junebugs dead in a shoe . dew-soaked on the porch

.

cat in the garden . sphinx-still in flustered flowers
on rusty pulleys . a clothesline two stories up
between a window . and a telephone pole dressed
toe to top in trumpet vine .

. clusters of roses
wrapped in plastic foil . confined to pickle buckets
one sand grain inside a shoe . worrying a foot
a three-legged chair . still serving as a plant stand

.

even the layers of paint . graining an old house
even the butterfly bush . bent down in hard rain
even the turtle's dull head . poking from the stream
every song says . tears represent a knowledge
for which anyone would trade . who knows only song

.

.

hasty note to self . never take your own advice
stylized plum blossoms . flattering white porcelain
bleed their darkest blue . imitating old tattoos
scribbled messages . not forgotten exactly
just left long enough . to summon other meanings

.

were I to worship a thing . instead of a name
I would praise this crude quetzal . carved from stone-black wood
polished down stone-smooth . its head cocked and curious

for I too wonder . what the world is like beyond
the trees of Guatemala . whether the flowers
carved on our bellies . always favor craved faces
and whether other small gods . have wings they can't use

.

.

if I knew his name . I would know why he did it
her last words to me .

. what I recall of the wreck
exactly like she used to .

. for those few moments
pursued obliquely .

. seen sideways and in shadow
I didn't get a clear look . it happened so fast

.

.

this map's measurements mimic . nothing in the world
the field's new furrows . follow the wandering gulch
sometimes sentences and lines . need to be the same
daughters suffocate . beneath their fallen fathers
anything you can explain . I don't need to hear

.

unpredictably angled . strings crisscross a grid
the three drunk boys tried . to beat the oncoming train
I trusted your character . enough to mar mine
my hopelessnesses . rooted firmly as tree stumps
it takes the platelets . and returns the red blood cells
they shouted warnings . before they fired on the crowd
I'm sorry okay . I didn't mean what I said

.

a three-legged dog . howls at his master's leaving
a woman snores in her first . sleep as a widow
a man shuffling papers looks . for a lost letter

not all songs are songs of joy . but all songs are songs
a child screams after a fall . not pain but surprise
.
.
I call old lovers . by my unborn daughters' names
Celeste Selene Sarah . *April Abandon*
my unborn daughters . I call by the Latin names
of garden perennials . *Hemerocallis*
Minuartia verna . *Convallaria*
.
my flowers I call . by the names of old lovers
because they speak the seasons . through their blossoming
because their roots survive snow .
. because hummingbirds
call forth their colors . this year as always before
Corinne I call one . *Luda* I call another
each name a previous life . *Grace Harmony Hope*
and emerald birds . fight to hear how they answer

The God of Window Screens and Honeysuckle

Summer

Suspended by one strand of spiderweb, seedburst
hovers and swings, counting out time, scribbling its sign
that this world is cursed with repletion, blessed with waste.
One wind shift, and light-gray fence rails darken with rain.
God gets to *assign* meaning to the three gray cats
crouched at an open door looking out through the screen,
to round rocks clattering, to the fly that insists
on entreating my right arm again and again.
Even dry months host a luxury of moonlight,
a sybaresis of dry leaves, of sprinkler spray
blown onto a neighbor's yard, of last plums picked at
by thirsty birds, paving stones tree roots lift and splay,
holes eaten into leaves at even intervals and straight,
sons following fathers, swinging their arms the same way.

1.

Reflected, a branch green as the original
hovers and swings, counting out time, scribbling a sign
on the window. On a panel truck visible
beyond the tree: GENTLE. Is it observation
to wait, eyes closed, in a dark room? alone? until
what? Is it observation not to? Even rain
this light, this half-willed, obligatory, partial,
the wind still intermittently blows to the screen.
To savor its flowering, the astilbe waits
one more day. Already bark has started to swallow
wire left touching the trunk. One stout canna sprout lifts
a clod like a storm-cellar door. Clearer, although
no louder: *Bob-white*. Someone has to think the thoughts
that happen in parts and cost a year to think through.

2.

The old man's left index finger bears a bent last
joint, but he still makes the bar chords. More evidence
for this world's curse of repletion, blessing of waste.
The blind boy beside him with a pack of Winstons
taps time to "Foggy Mountain Breakdown." A man stakes
a sign with his heel: *For Sale Rides Real Good*. Cell phones
through open windows, and a mockingbird imitates
their ringing. A box turtle gets stuck at a fence.
The grass has lost already but the war goes on
between clover and the dirt. Two rosy finches
bob to the seed with one rhythm. Lines of trees in
light fog at sunrise take on colors by distance:
green, blue, silver, white. And in Newark a dozen
ships' ghosts sunk in mud rust into dark outlines.

3.

First drops visible only as movement of leaves,
struck piano keys. Nothing terrifies more than
the long, layered responsibilities of love.
One wind shift makes light-gray fence rails darken with rain
that burdens the butterfly bush, bends it over
until it smothers coreopsis and lupine.
A motorboat's wake from ten thousand feet above:
thin wings, white bird on a blue flag, stylized airplane.
Things the understanding must forfeit to the body:
the lush last logic before sleep, the eyes' bee-dance,
a tin roof matching color with the twilit sky,
a deer in a clearing lifting her head from the grass,
honeysuckle's scent, a still heron, a wary
rabbit that watches you but will not meet your eyes.

4.

When I rock, the image in the double-paned glass
makes love to itself. I know the badly warped wood
that leaves long narrow pools on the drying deck says
I am lazy and the boards need to be replaced,
but God gets to mete out meaning to the three cats
always replacing each other in my back yard
while my bare-chested, beach-ball-bellied neighbor sits
on his riding mower, his son on his lap, bored.
To plant beside the creek: one of the small hostas
split from its parent plant last fall, the cider jar full
of pennies, browntone photos of the ruined house,
a marker for the dog, nicknames of friends from school,
books I should read but never will, our old mattress,
the hundred desires I can name but not fulfill.

5.

The will above the will, the will that scorns desire,
sings too, a countersong, continuo, droll drone
of the air conditioner beneath birds' chatter,
the pencil upstairs (vibrating to the door slammed down-)
that gives its coffee mug pitch, the purring observer,
crouched at an open door, looking out through the screen,
that watches its owner on her porch water
hanging flowers and toss their pruned leaves to the lawn.
After the patched pothole on the highway, dark stains
one tire's circumference apart grow rapidly
lighter and lighter. Nearby, fur around the wound's
edge on a roadkill carcass manifests decay
by turning black as range-fire grass. Crenellations
on a barn's roof prove roosting pigeons, spaced evenly.

6.

This week, sounds. Ping of aluminum baseball bats,
the black lab that fills a Sentra, its wagging tail
brushing the back seat, a skateboard's wheels and bearings,
its clatter when the boarder tries a trick but fails,
the graceless *oof* of a deer's hooves on our grass,
paper slid over metal getting out the mail,
small round rocks clattering, and the fly that insists
on circling, not caring how furiously I flail.
Give me to hear the wholly mundane, and see it.
Crack across a window in an arc, gapped with wear
from vibration. In a dock's wooden stanchions, cut
by a hawser, itself rubbed raw, a smooth groove. Air
rising from sidewalk grates at night, but also light.
Scaffolding over sidewalks. Bags on parking meters.

7.

Sunbather on elbows reading *The Sea, the Sea,*
or the woman in tights, their heelstrap loose behind
her ankles? Or is original sin more simply
that *nothing* fills the gap between desire and reason?
Rising, a scaled serpent from a yellow map's sea,
an exposed root, hunchbacked, forces the trail to bend.
God: nothing: quick twitching in the boy's wandering eye
that keeps meeting my eyes again and again.
Ideas gather as water gathers, and rise
as water rises, linger thin as dew on leaves,
as speckles of sap, or more heavily on cars,
pooled in huge drops on hoods and in streaks down windshields.
Sand in long, even streaks of brown on fresh-swept streets,
road stripes fanned by tire marks into egret feathers.

8.

A willow's long branches hang into the water
but do not spread as hair would. Nine Canada geese
float by, the wind at their backs lifting their feathers.
Upside down on gray wood racks, three yellow canoes
dangle frayed ropes. A boy on his father's shoulders
looks back at his mother. On the lake's ridged surface
a tree trunk obscured by branches finds a mirror.
Once upon a time, we did not need to choose.
Even dry months celebrate excess of moonlight,
of dust, attentive as new love, a thin white film
over your life, the two small marks darkening paint,
symmetrical arcs rubbed by corners of a frame.
Half-emptied, we sing as a wineglass sings at night,
a lover's finger lightly rubbed around its rim.

9.

The ospreys' constant cries: even the beautiful
and well-fed have grounds for lament. A strip of lead
meanders across a pane of old glass to fill
a crack. In the molding, one eye hook, painted
so often it's closed. Resonating through a hall
the gasps of strapping tape repeatedly unwound,
cut off, smoothed out. Leaning out over the trail
too far, a lowest branch by now completely stripped.
In summer this hot, what more can one wish for than
a sybaresis of dry leaves, of sprinkler spray
falling farther and farther behind, of the drone
from flies, bees, hummingbirds, cicadas, of two boys
with long-handled nets on their shoulders, looking down
into a stream, guessing if it's worth it to stay.

10.

And it *is* worth it. In divinity's absence
our world refuses to cull sacred from profane,
but does evoke and nourish more, and more intense,
attention than we can sustain. To a broken
beer bottle whose label holds brown shattered fragments
together, to the greenredyellowblue garden
animated by two white butterflies, to pigeons
flashing into flight, bright backs no longer hidden,
to dew on a car's hood x-raying its structure,
to the sound of a duffel bag's strap, to the chair
blown down in a neighbor's yard, to plums picked over
by blue jays, to two snow geese preening near the shore
on a rock too small for them, to chalk dust *under*
blackboard trim, to death's order: flies, leather, sawdust, air.

11.

Five trucks on one another's backs, five turtles
sunning on a log. One ice truck taller than wide
or long shakes to a stop, then shakes starting, then stalls.
A boy on a bike pulls a boy on a skateboard
who keeps shouting *Faster, faster!* until he falls.
Once a bridge, now equidistant isolated pads
of concrete, square islands populated by gulls.
Thought's erratic flight: more butterfly than bird.
Black-eyed Susans grown through a fence mimic the sun.
Wings together straight up, the resting butterfly
becomes a sailboat, black and white, yellow and brown.
Roosting birds shit on paving stones roots lift and splay.
The first yellow leaf: one light on at night in town.
Seven orange balls on wire lined across the sky.

12.

Substitutes for joy: sloped sound of cutting open
a cantaloupe; smoke smell from next door's charcoal grill
selling summer by evoking recollection
of winter chimneys; season's first hummingbird, still
visiting weeks later; basset hound lying on
her side, snoring; fleeting false-autumn morning chill;
a spiderweb glowing at night; tea before dawn;
stone that has replaced a fallen tree, cell by cell;
one layer of clouds racing another, both moonlit;
cows cooling in a farm pond, each up to its neck;
the house's afternoon shadow, its edge still hot;
reticent edges of pages in a new book;
holes eaten into leaves at even intervals and straight;
a square section bitten from one wing of a monarch.

13.

Suspended by a strand of spiderweb, seedburst
still flies, but flies in place. So many tragedies
without recognition scenes. Folded in like bats,
dried leaves hang in clusters. On black butterfly wings,
yellow meanders mimic EKG charts.
Hay bales, barrels scattered from a wrecked train. Gold leaves'
rocking fall, cicadas' circular sound, in contrast
to the sun's straight descent. Dried blooms on the cannas.
Two women, taking their time, walking stride for stride,
even turning their heads together, see the city.
First a boy's arm through the fence to his shoulder, stretched
toward a dog, then the same dog, no longer shy,
her head through to her collar on the other side.
Sons follow their fathers, swing the same arms, the same way.

Fall

Rusting bulldozer, rusting wellhead and backhoe,
rusting LTD. One last hummingbird, rust-necked,
trusts red among rusting cannas. Through the window,
a voice calling *Come on back, that's it, come on back,*
a swingset's rusty voice severed by a chainsaw,
then, thinned by the mile from the road to here, a truck
gearing down. Just briefly, a cluster of sparrows
musters on the screen, each bird clinging, feet and beak,
caught between the mute inward spiral and the one
that speaks, between those dead leaves that as they fall
tap the dying to follow and the yellow-brown
dying that argue among themselves how to call
the dead back, between the pepper blushing top-down
and the buddleia's brown base erasing purple.

14.

Hard to believe someone once drove, once nicknamed, this
rusting LTD that the hummingbirds, rust-necked,
mock with their flight, that crabgrass and thistles caress.
Someone planted these sunflowers, each fist-sized head flecked
with yellow stipples like straight pins coiled in circles.
And these cannas whose broad leaves in raw wind affect
sculler's oars but faster, a tightrope walker's arms.
Clematis bending a branch to pull itself erect.
Ideas occur between beliefs, in the gaps
they leave exposed. The hammer's yellow handle moves
out of sync with its echoes off nearby houses.
Atop the squared-off evergreen bush, its trimmings
turning brown. Any one world calls out to others.
A plane sifts its dusty frosting onto plowed fields.

15.

Substitutes for sorrow: a kink in the garden hose;
hungry bees and hummingbirds that even this late
seek red among rusting cannas; on the fencerow
a spot of soft light that changes shape, its movement
mapping the one small gap in the maple's shadow;
illuminated by intense stadium lights,
a swirling mist anticipating blowing snow;
strips of tar across the road to patch the asphalt;
leaves that fall to the seat of the patio swing
as goldfinches, still luminous, fall to the feeder;
seeing the year's last hummingbird, without knowing;
circling an idea, unable to land there;
ditch so dry its algae patch is cracked and flaking;
the neighbor's old dog, who can't hear or remember.

16.

So long has this dry spell lasted that just one rain
will not swell the earth enough to seal all its cracks.
God: nothing: the leaves' deep last green before they turn,
a voice calling *Come on back, that's it, come on back.*
At least ten feet off the ground on a window screen
a grasshopper pauses, facing down. *Propane tanks
filled here,* or the more common, less legible signs
left by writhers who live their whole lives under rocks.
Beside our open bedroom windows, houseplants stir
from desire or sympathy or recollection.
What more do we know beyond ourselves than weather?
We would have to believe our beliefs more than we can
to believe them as we should. The brightest morning star:
an airplane on its approach, miles away, before dawn.

17.

A hedgeapple falling, the neighbor's radio,
a rusty squeaking roof vent, someone yelling *You boys*
stop that, cicadas, cars on the highway, sparrows
rustling in gutters: all these competing noises.
A swingset's rusty voice severed by a chainsaw.
One life nourished by the erotic, one poisoned.
Though latched shut and locked, the truck's draw-down trailer door
each time it takes a bump clatters and tries to rise.
Two screens between us gray the neighbor's white lace curtains,
but the sun makes pumpkin-colored soy fields brighter
now than our maple will be. Though it clings to green,
gold has found at branch's end one eight-leaf cluster.
The horizon approaches, and rising mountains
make everything else grow narrow and more clear.

18.

Scott's Home Furnishings. Entering St. Clair County.
Every third phone pole, one more insulator, hooked
to a ground. *American Dream. Ozark Novelties.*
At the limestone quarry, a flatbed trailer stacked
with empty pallets. *One Hundred Varieties.*
Then, a mile up the road from here, lights of a truck
crest the hill. Cable ends bundled like grain sheaves rise
from a trench. *Richardson's Country Crafts. Shuteye Creek.*
God: nothing: sidewalk patch made odd-colored by rain,
song of moonscape's sleep, lava crunching underfoot,
black wingtips on white pelicans in formation,
a yellow plastic children's slide the next day, wet
with neglect but shining, gray shingles dried to brown.
In the lake a thousand stumps and one white egret.

19.

Why would my caressing the backs of other worlds
diminish my love for this one? The wordless heat
of the body, or the mumbling cold of the mind.
What measurement more accurate or more patient
than fence rails in mist darkening down? Where leaves land
when they fall, and the melodies they intuit
strumming the tightly strung, long-past flight paths of birds.
Generous moon, with Venus shining to match it,
ardently attentive to the world, like a cat
worshipping birds. Flicker on a branch stump, leaning
over, pecking upside down. From a bluff's dry dirt,
growing horizontally, fifty red saplings.
Leaning from the garbage truck as from a sailboat.
Though the gods no longer speak to us, they still sing.

20.

In a stand of maples, a solitary pine,
its predatory angel a white-breasted hawk.
One sunflower stem cut through: a giant hardened
artery, lined with a black-crusted brittle plaque.
A rotting tomato's white fibrous spiderweb wound.
Dead grass in the compost turned silver and black
as if it had been burning. Blooms brown and shrunken.
Birds on the screen, each clinging with its feet and beak.
God: nothing: one plum still clinging as the leaves fall.
The raccoon's panic, too late to flee the headlights.
Hard-packed, clay-dense soil that resists root and shovel
but still crumbles in the fist. In two small buckets,
iris bulbs like crayfish. Burrowing into tall
grass, leaves gone off one by one to die by themselves.

21.

Catalog: heard before dawn, but smothered by day;
seen in season, but hidden the rest of the year;
overlooked in itself, but seen some other way;
not pursued, but waited on, overheard, watched for;
one woman whistling dogs home, one checking the mail.
Where one thought has fallen, another will flower.
Three hundred fence rails in a line, one warped away.
Diamonds quilted on a trailer's aluminum door.
Caught between the mute inward spiral that draws down
and the outward spiral that draws up, draws dizzy,
the harvest continues at night: from the combine
corn thrown down into the truck avoids the frenzy
of chaff like bugs swirling around the floodlight. Moons,
planets, stars in a tiny fugitive galaxy.

22.

With a rhythmic rustle, leaves being raked defy
their own rule: shh, shh. Irregular leopard-spot
circles blemish them. Twine, black from twenty years' stay
underground, but still too strong for the spade to cut.
Does discipline learn more than the senses set free?
Turned mirror at dawn, east-facing windows compete
with sun and trees for gold. A tomato's husk, dry,
flimsy as paper, litters the turned garden dirt.
This time of year it is the farmhouse falling down
that speaks, between dead leaves blown into ragged piles
like brown snowdrifts in corners and against rotten
planters upset on the porch, and the vapor trail
that at dawn spreads wide between Venus and the moon:
roof sagging, in place of the door a plywood panel.

23.

First leaves get collected, then full garbage bags fall
from a pickup, forcing cars to swerve around them.
Above the rooftops, the only leaves visible
make a squirrel's nest. Around the base of the elm
swirling wind has swept clear a bare, leaf-free circle.
God: nothing: boy walking home, jacket on his arm.
Sunflower's stem tilted but propped by its rootball.
Last night's rain collected in a cut canna stem.
You cannot watch too carefully or wait too long
for the idea that will change your life, that will
tap you, dying, to follow the yellow-brown
leaves in their going, no longer the anxious child
stamping one foot while his mother ties the shoestring
on the other. No longer hungry, not yet full.

24.

God: nothing: burnished streaks from fittings on the wing.
The height we name flight, watching from the ocean floor.
A raven settling on a streetlight but rising
as six startled starlings. Under the eaves, hardly more
than a wisp, a wasp nest. A seagull bullying
fully thirty pigeons for half an apple core.
In a grassy field a capped pipe joined to nothing,
wanting, as we do, what it lacks preconditions for.
Like old neglected barns buckling, leaving only
sunstreaks and swallows and mice and an owl, we fall
into our worst ideas, imitate the noisy
dying who argue among themselves what to call
the horizon, naming frustration, like the fly,
with an incessant, futile buzzing at the sill.

25.

Fifteen geese descend to the lake through a thousand
blackbirds scattering. Bare branches in the valley
rise from the fog, black racks of antlers on a herd
of white elk. At dusk blackbirds bloom on our bare trees
like upside-down leaves. I want ideas I can *hold*
without believing them. Four leaves on the driveway,
three pieces of gravel, one twig. Between gusts, the sound
of sparrows cracking seeds, a sprinkler rattling leaves.
At dawn the burner's blue flame glows outside and in,
and downed leaves tumbling in wind feign wounds, mock injured
birds deprived of flight that parent birds abandon,
call forth dream and memory, make me want to lure
the dead back, even when the pepper's blushing top down
has told me to ready the garden for winter.

26.

Rusting bulldozer, rusting wellhead and backhoe,
darkened, like everything else, by rain: stained driveway
and sidewalks, tree trunks, fallen leaves, one laceless shoe,
a length of downspout and a blown-over chair that lie
on the grass. Down a marsh hawk's breast, brown stars in rows
that rise with her. An owl will swoop down and away
from the same branch in dark silhouette tomorrow
when the moon's huge ring haloes the house and the tree.
What we see we see as beginnings and endings,
so we save no names for events in the middle,
for the hanging flower basket's lazy swaying
beside furious wind chimes, for two merged puddles
under the basketball goal after frost's melting,
for the buddleia's brown base erasing purple.

Winter

Stubble rows, four matte, four shiny in morning sun,
record the combine's turnings. What can be preserved
must be preserved as some self other than its own.
Bent cattails mimic stubble in the frozen pond.
Suet nearly gone, chickadees cling upside down
to the feeder. Above it, a hedgeapple wedged
between branches since fall. Past that, changing direction
at once like a shoal of krill, a thousand blackbirds.
Skaters on a pond, we fall into what we know,
drown in disorienting light before we freeze.
In angled afternoon sun, the fence's shadow
caresses the snow's contours like tight-fitting clothes.
Even when grass greens, reenacting spring, the snow
will linger, longest in the shadows of houses.

27.

Dead hosta leaves dried to yellow-brown all lie down
in a single direction. What can be preserved
has been. A mop bleached white set to dry in the sun.
Through the fence and even the thin cedar, a road
turned chickadee gray. What else? Anything that can
be lost is luxury, and what does that exclude?
Not the clouds that look today like corrugation.
Not the L gouged in a dry lake being strip-mined.
Tiny sparks flash from a pickup's studded snow tires
on the highway at night. In a curtained window
a silhouette lives its moth-life. A day changes
its name, a life its purpose, a death its tableau.
God: nothing: faucet drip-dripping in a still house.
Tree on a hillside, fruit lined at the fence below.

28.

Strong wind: insubstantial, dangerous, unbidden.
To grow as subtly varied as prairie, a mind
must be preserved as some self other than its own,
must learn to long for lightning, to be restored
by periodic fires, but it must also learn
patience like the plum tree's: snow in its abandoned
nest, but still bearing withered fruit on limbs barren
of leaves, like remnants of weeds where our flowers failed.
Still expecting scraps at the neglected feeder
a nuthatch returns again and again. Grown back
six inches since they were trimmed, iris leaves appear
above the snow. Four chairs stacked on the neighbor's deck.
Next right: Hay for Sale: 858-9024.
Furrows filled with snow: stripes down the breast of a hawk.

29.

Grass this morning stays frost-silvered six inches past
the house's receding shadow. The evening sun
sets at the exact angle the neighbor's roof slants.
Bent cattails mimic stubble in the frozen pond.
Black trash bags wear one white stripe where the sun reflects.
Bromegrass slow dances with her lover, the breeze. One
junco's white tailfeather is longer than the rest.
God: nothing: one string giving the other five sound.
Sliding lock on the frame, no matching hasp on the door.
Soccer balls rest at the fence, the yard's lowest point.
Any night sky wants wanderers through its fixed stars.
As sleet melts onto pavement, lines of light pivot.
Watch expectantly to see precisely what is here.
Listen patiently to hear precisely what is not.

30.

An artificial rose left lying on a lawn
tells winter's lie about summer. In thin layer
snow marks the elm's trunk like birch bark. Topo lines
map a puddle as if it froze while someone stirred.
Suet nearly gone, chickadees cling upside down
to the feeder, wearing the colors of winter:
wing feathers gray like shingles or dirty snow, crown
wet-asphalt black, breast the hazy white of cloud cover.
In an inverted V, starlings outline a roof
as if they were carved on it. A pear, half eaten,
left on a window ledge, frozen now, shines, glazed smooth.
God: nothing: snow showing where each roof gets no sun.
Hours treated like seeds that, tended, might bear fruit.
Vacant car wash: three cathedral arches, in tin.

31.

A woman lets out her dog, walks out in houseshoes
and plaid shorts despite the cold, her wet hair turbaned
in a red towel, to pick up her paper. Grass
shines, foil under frost that silvers even cardboard
and a wadded Dentyne wrapper. Sparrows take turns
at the feeder. Above it, a hedgeapple wedged
in the ramage will fall next year, after it rots.
A nine of hearts waits, lost in leaves beside the road.
Nine reflector dots compose an orange diamond,
one two three two one. Tilled soil, caramel-colored
with patches the brown of bread crust, surrounds a pond.
Crossing an overpass, a motorcyclist's head,
disembodied. Looped back onto itself, one strand
of cable dangles. Mind: not empty, but emptied.

32.

Light leaves afterimages for the retina;
words, echoes for the mind. Dry snow mimics wet sand
windblown in terraces ragged as marble's veins,
skittish juncos' tracks scratch the snow to patina.
Magnified by melting, cat tracks in the snow end
mysteriously, with nowhere to jump. Doves descend
between branches to food scattered in all directions,
thistleseed like geese sleeping on a frozen pond.
These protestations permit me to disobey
the sybaritic intelligence of the hands.
Days after the storm, snow still swirls on the highway
like smoke rising. Vertical gaps between shingles,
horizontal black. Thermal panes host frost only
where their false lattice mimics our old, drafty house.

33.

Haloing a fallen hedgeapple, snow assumes
its shape without touching it. Formed on layers
of exposed rock, ice mimics limestone shapes in caves.
Wind-smoothed and sunlight-softened into sloped hollows,
once-crisp tracks in snow slowly decay. In loose loops,
three different garden hoses crown the neighbor's fence.
The chaotic swarm descending onto phone lines
at once becomes parallel, a thousand blackbirds.
Stuck to the pyramid-shaped top of each fence post,
snow marks the east and south slopes. Suet: flicker, then
starlings, woodpeckers, then chickadees, smallest last.
At the gutter's seam, a long icicle points down
to a small, mirror-smooth ice patch. Not the mind first.
Better a tragic death than a merciful one.

34.

Late this lisped afternoon fringes of clouds that hid
the sun grow brighter than the sun itself. Risen
in clusters from the frozen lake, agitated,
negotiating geese haggle a ragged line.
Tomorrow at dawn the cornstubble, frost-covered,
will look like fields full of foam when you face the sun,
like velvet when you face away. Raising a dustcloud,
a horse rolls on her back and gallops upside down.
Skaters on a pond, we fall into what we know,
drawn down easily as eyes are drawn to motion,
birds and stormclouds and sunsets in preference to
the tree trunk that would better test our attention,
turned earth patterned like woodpeckers' wings by the snow,
the clay flowerpot on its side reddened by rain.

35.

The steeping teabag floats, borne by an air pocket
shaped like a heart. Thursday noon at the church, no one
to turn off its porch light. Washed-out gray-white leaves float
on black mud beside the curb where the yard drains down.
Brittle black candlewicks curl; new white wicks stand straight.
A chipped PVC pipe's rough chalky fracture line
mimics a fresh-calved iceberg's surface. Tree trunk cut
thigh-size hangs on the wire fence to which it had grown.
The same breath-brief bodies that bind us to the land
drown us in disorienting light, leave us to freeze
in open sea, suffocate in space, abandoned.
The less reassuring calls forth strong resistance
from the more. A factory twenty miles distant:
blue against the pink sunrise, smokestack steam rises.

36.

Evening, and cows gather at the metal gate
that leads to the barn. Even this late in winter
brown leaves still cling to some trees and swirl in the street.
Candles on a child's cake, two-foot-high cedars
decorate a yellow field. Scouring the grass, eight
mourning doves, then ten: always an even number.
Against the windows periodic bursts of sleet
but on the roof a quieter, steadier patter.
Its movement has slowed after the first allegro,
but from the cellist's bow one worn horsehair dangles.
In angled afternoon sun, the fence's shadow
strains for the house. The shadow of a white candle
says solid, but gets defied by the sun shining through.
My failure: I see things with names: fence, window, wall.

37.

A hungry cat watching a bird, all attention,
a man watching women after receiving a note
signed *Secret Admirer*. To see four power lines
strung pole to pole, the lowest looser than the rest;
of the dormant hosta in the garden, that one
brown stem stands petals intact, one bends at the waist;
one cinder-block strip in layers of brown sandstone;
the thin sheet of ice freezing the compost bin shut.
A truck approaches, announced first by trembling ground.
A raven rises, its head white as an eagle's.
Despite the spirit. At home. A sensual wind
caresses snow's contours, a hand under a blouse.
Then the thaw. By the fence in the lumberyard
damp pallets stacked seven high in crooked rows.

38.

Wind ripples melted snow held by surface tension
on the glass-topped patio table. A farmyard's
sodium light lit so early this afternoon
signals another storm, as do hedgeapple limbs
swinging the feeders and groaning their homely tune.
A candy wrapper blows past their roots, a rag waves
from branches to assert that tomorrow at dawn
for one moment the sky's blue will match the river's.
One paint can in the row that fills the barn's window
tilts, leaning on the rest. An hour's observation
of one view from one place daily, attended to,
offers plenty to stock an imagination.
Soon enough, grass will green in hope of spring, but snow
will take its turn, first to suffer transformation.

39.

Stubble rows, four matte, four shiny in morning sun
will be plowed under soon. Light seeps across the sky,
spilled water wicking through cloth, and glimmers in
water standing in truck tracks in mud. Ivory
in most light, the vinyl blinds turn rosy at dawn.
A horse's coat, the wet street turns black and glossy.
The gutter has caught a fallen window screen.
Flirt with perception, yes, but kiss her, warily.
A god who motivates prayers need not answer them.
One scrawled onto scrolls, woven into tapestries,
incised onto stone need not speak. Flaking paint trims,
where water carries structure down, a grid of cracks.
Snowflakes darken mulch, melting from their blue-white bloom,
but they live longest in the shadows of houses.

Spring

Five first crocuses burst into bird-brilliant bloom
and suddenly everything flies: behind a car
scraps of paper rise, two from a flock, startled dumb.
Some lives begin in abstraction; others end there.
Could I find the child's fist this universe bloomed from
I would close it again as my own five fingers,
say worlds as one sentence, fit them into a name
for gold overwhelming finches, feather by feather.
With leaves returned, we still hear birds but see them now
only when they fly. It's hard to *see* anything,
even when we hear it sing, even though we know
it's there, even if we feel it filling our lungs.
Forsythia insists all that is is yellow.
None of this had to happen, but it had to be sung.

40.

This southerly sun casts shadows even at noon,
and under it everything flies: the tops of cars
like waterbugs skim the surface of a fence line.
Titmice wait skittishly for the rosy finches
to finish at the feeder. Gently kiss reason,
kiss intuition hard. Five closed-up crocuses,
bright crepe-paper rolls, unfurled today in the sun.
Who would want a love that arose from pure motives?
With no birds on them and a cold front passing through,
naked limbs click their wooden windsong to themselves
as clouds gather a gradually deeper blue.
On the copper bottom of a steel pot, rainbows.
Even a wrong course one sometimes ought to pursue
to its end, till refusal of praise becomes praise.

41.

Water stretched across the squares of a window screen
gives it compound eyes. Not until the screen dries will
scraps of paper rise, birds in a flock, from the ground.
Light limits the kind of clarity possible,
as when yellow light from a streetlamp shining down
on trees makes wet limbs look icy, or the apple,
tricked into blossom, begs for one last lie from the sun
for its blooms, cotton pulled from an aspirin bottle.
When you depart for the desert may matter more
than when, or whether, you return. How deep your roots
may tell how rare and luminous your blooms. Each square
on the wet sidewalk dries from its edges in. Sleet's
patter has tiny hooves. I like the world better
in the wet screen, so complete in so many dots.

42.

What could bring consolation except artifice?
How much could the cause of sadness really matter?
One leaf, left back, flips over but stays, hooked in grass.
Some lives that start in abstraction also end there.
Angered by gusts from a gathering storm, branches
of trees turn rivals, rut-bold bucks locking antlers.
After rain, waterbeads world-full as blackbirds' eyes,
bright as noon sun, goosebump the arms of a lawn chair.
Premonitions: often earned, but seldom given.
A lone chickadee tries each neglected feeder,
sunflower first, then suet, then seed, then he's gone.
Ideas repeat like fragments of tunes. Over
beaver mounds rounded out of the roadside marsh one
red-winged blackbird flies, light as a lover's finger.

43.

Intuitions bloom from the life that precedes them,
glow, like daffodils, golden even in darkness,
make their own light like the purple and green that gleam
in glyphs on the slick black neck feathers of grackles.
Could I find the child's fist this universe bloomed from
I would force it back into a single sentence.
Red tulips wither toward their fifty-week home,
darkening back to its color: binge and penance.
Penance and binge: one day of sunshine, one of rain
and the grim world goes green again. This world that takes
back its gifts just gave me one. Through linen curtains
thin light whispers how thin the moon through thin clouds looks.
A girl in a red jacket, swinging, pleads *Come on!*
to her father while he laughs and leans on his rake.

44.

How to sever myself from my own experience
in a way that also severs others from theirs,
to start out gold like new green leaves on old willows,
like fire hydrants painted to predict daffodils,
to open out the world as a bird unfurls wings,
then enfist it again in my ill-formed fingers,
to lean impossibly far over the world as
over a drainage channel a bare tree teeters.
Sometimes resistance itself must be resisted.
Empty swing rocking, wind its imagination.
On last year's rose cane, one dried leaf, a tiny bird.
This year's first moth has found the porch light, the door screen.
The roof's frost melts first in even stripes above studs.
God: nothing: last thoughts of a woman dying alone.

45.

One thick branch blown down, yes, but a thousand blossoms
plucked one by one by the rain surround and cover it.
A thousand droplets from the humid, breath-warm room,
ideas condense on windows, filtering light,
not curving, the sharp shadows from a window frame,
following folds across curtains but opposite
the weave. Worlds named in sentences, sentenced to names.
A low ridge of rocks combs the shallow river white.
God: nothing: brightness left out when we name the sky's hue.
Under composting cannas a nest of rabbits,
one more honoring of instinct, hiding from view,
huddling against the cold. Geese shimmying breast-first
onto the shore. Two men in a field, wearing blue,
facing the same direction, standing hands on hips.

46.

On its brief bursts branch to branch, a bird loops below
then rises above in a sine curve. A border
collie sprints around a horse whose hooves make an o
in the mud to stay facing him. Later, neighbors'
lights stretch curb to curb, reflected on the wet road.
On a robin's tail one unpaired white eye wonders
how far to the sky. Dandelion angels float
while gold overwhelms the finches, feather by feather.
Some mornings I wake early, terrified of one
particular thought; some nights I stay up late,
terrified of thought itself. A far flag stirs, then
nearer flowers, then our trees, as a manifest
but invisible approaches, a stronger than
solid, the unappeasable for which I wait.

47.

Distorted by distance and wind, dogs' barking sounds
like the crying of migrating geese. History,
topography: sediment rings mark depressions
in a flat roof's tarpaper. How could we not see
failure coming? Leaks forming, shingle-sided sheds
wilting, set here how?, leaning on fences, tipsy.
God: nothing: sunflower husks strewn by careless birds.
Bark in long strips peeling away from a dead tree.
With leaves returned, we still hear birds but see them now
only after tired clouds, emptied to zinc, give their
last sheet-metal thunder, and the sated grass glows.
Power lines rivaling greening trees rise over
them at each pole, then sink. Migratory birds know
well the horizon's pull, but we know it better.

48.

A dozen white blooms linger past their prime on top
of a plum tree, ideas we once believed in,
cars coasting downhill on a wet road, tires' hiss sharp
as tearing paper, a steep roof's shingles drying down,
a face slowly going pale. Ideas, made not
of mind but of words, thus mimic mind itself. Sun
will keep finding exposed rock though the seepage stop
soaking the strata below it days after rain.
Before dawn, names gather in the trees, a chorus,
but after they fly it's hard to see anything
anymore. Their echoes, like the smell of cut grass,
linger, as do their remnants, grass clippings floating
in a puddle, after rain a thousand seed strips
imitating earthworms on the driveway drying.

49.

A cat the color of dryer lint perches on
the garden's wood trim, watching birds, perfectly still,
driven to kill by envy, not hunger. Deeper than
the morning sky is bright, late evening sky can call
forth new hues, willing the white barn blue. The old barn,
back sagging, gray-brown boards warped and buckling, models
the horses it once housed. Facing the wind, poised on
a fencepost, a robin flares its wingtips and tail.
One broken branch hangs, wavers between stay and go.
An idea can hide, perfectly transparent,
even when we hear it sing, even though we know
it's there, even if it looms over us, a threat,
the way grass shaped like a breaking wave threatens to
slip off the lip of a steep eroded embankment.

50.

Her stroller seat faces backward, so the small girl
strains to turn around, to see what her mother sees,
suffer sight first, not feeling. In the compost pile
a measured scratching mimics footsteps on dry leaves.
Beak pointed skyward, head cocked back, a male grackle
struts. When he calls clouds away from the sun, the trees
lengthen across the lawn. In glass at this angle
the dried bouquet of tea-rose buds reflects, colorless.
What should be my preoccupations, if not these?
Desire cannot be made sessile, though like pigeons
it can learn to home. Nameless, mostly, but always
there. Always, always we feel it filling our lungs,
in, out, out, in. Mine, today: two windows, four trees,
six goldfinches. Enough to sustain anyone.

51.

Almost bouncing up, lighter for his load, a hawk,
his prey taken, lifts. The stepfather and stepson
down the street fight outside: *You attacked me you fuck*
you attacked a kid. On a phone line the falcon
bends to its prey again and again, kissing, lovestruck.
The father takes his turn shouting as the son runs
off. He knows the boy will return, will learn to pluck
some life from the barren, call his hunger devotion.
A line of grass glints, shows where I missed when I mowed.
Birds' path past the house, mapped by shit streaks on the drive.
In a field in bright sun, twenty round hay bales glow,
ten on each side of a creek, lined in rows of five.
Forsythia insists all that is is yellow.
Who would argue with that? What's not to believe?

52.

Five first crocuses burst into bird-brilliant bloom
weeks ago. I was watching then. I remember,
though they don't. God: nothing: a familiar song from
I know not what bird. How many crocuses? Where?
This year how many brittle bird-beaks of vellum
did I leave, plucking each iris when it withered?
How many fossil wheel-tracks will I leave in clumps
of sticky grass coughed out by the mulching mower?
Voracious spirits speak softly of the spirit
and sideways and seldom, but they speak. Fluttering
its wings, a baby robin follows its parent.
At a stoplight, a dog in a pickup, wagging
its tail, runs back to prop two paws on the tailgate.
Just what least needs to happen most needs to be sung.

REMARKS ON COLOR

•

Boy meets girl, girl smiles.
Boy colors, looks down.
I see music, a colored medium
that darkens its surroundings.
Her bright body the iris,
his dark mind the pupil.
He hears the night as dark,
she sees it as a medium.

•

Red-brown in daybreak's red-brown light
a dolor of doves pavanes on the lawn
under capricious trees,
but here color loves the evening,
always and only in secret,
withdrawn, watching from a distance
a brazen taint of starlings
brag its black advances.

•

Walking in the woods alone,
worrying a lantern,
abstracting everything, searching for you—
a color shines in darkness—
I passed a pond. Three men
stopped fishing to chase me
and I ran and ran and ran
but my fear was for you.

•

After first shy fascination becomes
the primordial relationship,
position, look at your room

late in mathematics
in asymptotic light.
Any form may appear human
when you can hardly see color,
when the rules decide they want you.

•

Doesn't white erase importance?
How important can one glance be?
A glance can be stolen, but from whom?
Stolen fire burns hottest.
Windburn, sunburn, snowblindness.
Blind singer's song, blind lover's touch.
Close your eyes and touch me there.
Am I the broad line your touch erases?

•

I wanted to smudge you my number
but could dream no pen, no paper.
Our sleep sleeps the question of color,
we who want, we who veil.
You were backing slowly away,
slurring into someone else.
I knew you would not return.
I knew you, but not myself.

•

What feeling unhinges the concept
of saturated color?
What names the crease
behind your knees? the skin on your knuckles?
the way my hand rests on your waist
when you lie on your side?
the whorls at the small of your back?
Can we say what surrounds us now?

•

Whiter love provokes brighter lusts.
Do you know what 'reddish' means?
On your body? On another's?
Is it better not to know?
Can you find it on me?
Where else have you looked?
Should I apply to the stars
what you told me of the moon?

•

Blue obliterates yellow.
The moon replaces the sun.
Winter makes even stars cold.
Blue insists on opposition.
I fell in love with the cold you,
your restless wanderers blue
among your cold blue stars,
each pursuing perfect isolation.

•

He calls love the abstraction that counts.
She says love is no abstraction.
He wishes she didn't know he knew
no direct route blue to yellow.
She hums the subject retrograde.
He thinks what he feels may be love.
She feels no need to think.
Portraits are landscapes, more or less veiled.

•

Felled, shredded, soaked to paper,
screened, sedimented, felted, layered
by your knowing hands that drowned
in daydown dull dualities,
all colors from collapsed to collapsed,
I fell in love with the ways I might die,

the elements that might consume me,
earth, water, fire, you.

·

When we love we love color,
the engauzing of our gaze
by lust-lisped inexplicabilities.
Cloudiness cannot tell red from green
and knows better than to try.
My love for you assumes
first the color of sawdust,
then the shade of a milk snake's shed skin.

·

I lose luminosity
whenever I dream of you
and I always dream of you
though colors cringe forth causes
and causes submerge me
so I can't surface
unless sun-conscious radiation
charges my dream-colored drowning.

·

I accept the censure
of your life's ravenous colors:
the oily sheen of beetles' backs
leaving a deer's eye sockets,
your aura when you trace
the circle of darkened fur
outlining its open belly
and turn to look back at me.

·

Don't forget that transparency
and gray can both be painted,
though not with transparent paint.

Don't forget that as years get shorter
love matters more but the lover less.
Don't forget the palpable can be abstract.
Don't forget you can lie about love
to your lover, or to yourself.

•

What makes bright colors differ?
He says one thing, she says another.
How does saturation feel?
He thinks he knows, she thinks he doesn't.
Why does one color's advance
return others to broad contour?
He thinks it is not one color.
She thinks the other colors merge.

•

Don't tell me there is no such thing
as luminous properties.
I feel them when you close my eyes,
when my hands, alive through light, wander
over your shoulders, your neck,
across your belly, behind your knees,
down your forearm elbow to wrist.
Your ankles glow, your shoulderblades shine.

•

I couldn't understand
how you could laugh underwater
or why you kept pulling me down.
The implied, we see abstractly.
Colors impose qualities and effects.
You hued vivid yellow-green.
Or she did who looked like you
in the boat, just out of my reach.

•

When you go, at night in my room
the particular falls away
and objects of luminous colors,
opalescent jellyfish
a mile below the surface,
drift, abstract in the cold current,
viscous stars thrown off
by a dissolving galaxy.

•

Confined so long in one frame,
me mocking your movements you mocking mine,
we plotted our environment
according to the story color told us,
the story of definite darkness,
brownian movement, expanding space,
suns burned out before our birth,
dancers dancing past closing time.

•

Love means the soul only pivots.
All names stand to be erased.
I knew it would before it did.
This visible life conceals others.
Line and color trust general truths.
A dark red can be blue too. Is.
What I say of someone else
hues itself true of you.

•

My hands that once pled color
now tighten to fetal fists.
No more cello, no more rocks
rounded by rivers, warmed by the sun,
no more tautening to the absolute,
touching one of your nipples

with my outstretched ring finger
and the other with my thumb.

•

These oblongs of light I take
as messengers, you as their message.
I watch them. I hear them say you,
hear how they cover your compulsion
to express the absolute.
Is red lighter than yellow?
I don't know. I resonate
at what pitch your tautness tells me to.

•

Your life looms over my life.
I hear you, but I can't find you.
Everything I made I made as gifts.
Do we share a shared emotion?
I watch for your visit, bird.
When you go, leave me your shadow.
The shadow white casts is gray.
Sometimes I can't tell which one is you.

•

I may be introverted but.
There are various definitions of.
I always wanted to with.
Additionally the light.
If only I had listened when.
Long ago I gave up trying to.
No one says of pure colors what.
When we do I imagine you as.

•

Your doing what you did to me
slowed the train plenty
though the grade stayed imperceptible.

What did you not do to me?
Which is odder: to call brown solid,
or say you love only me?
One color exists through another.
The ice melted, but froze again.

          •

Because the stars knew snow was coming
and that our firewood could not last
I was frantic to show you
I could pass through walls
and that white cancels all reflection
but ice formed inside the windows
and you cried because my fetching wood
left only the two of you.

          •

If we get in trouble it's your fault.
That we haven't yet is mine.
Why do I never fulfill
desires as simple as these?
Shape, movement, a little color,
our inner tragic pushing order out.
I mean more than I can say aloud.
And other. Why is there no gray light?

          •

What scared me was not the being on fire
but that all I touched began to burn,
that I made grief material.
Light licked from my luminous hand,
and I backed away from your approach,
throwing down books to slow you
but you ate them and their flames
shone yellow-green in your eyes.

          •

Floured palms dimpling dough,
one pair of lips against another,
ice melting off branches onto snow,
ice shaping rock for a million years.
Now I feel the abstract
as the impression of color,
the hole a rootball leaves
when a leaning life falls.

•

Try to paint what you see
when you see through my eyes
as once I saw through yours.
I want now only to remember
color purely seen, looking into them,
watching from outside at night
two women in a lighted room
lilting rum and laughing.

•

In place of lesser abstractions
I wonder now only about love,
about how to paint this graying light,
how to say into this darkening
any name your name might answer to,
how to call from this shade the shade,
beautiful but never touched,
who once was with me, or might have been.

Eighteen Maniacs

Please Say You Will

Voodoo	|	Dream do the rain or am I drink it? Keep secret your sun-squinted hues. Deeper disclosures drain down spilled colors clouds couldn't kept.
Felicity	|	One round earring same size as your world mind-wide from one same size as mine.
Stoptime	|	Gone mother underground gone somewhere other, gone measure, gone melody.
Syphilis	|	Smaller bear-brother, caught kin, mask-marked one, meander of tracks memorial in morning mud.
Peacherine	|	You'd laugh if I tolja.
Treemonisha	|	I know just what you means.
Swipesy	|	When I looked up, the back window bare black that watched the woods that had held purple-green, deer-dark, dim-but-stippled-still until I looked down.

Rabbit Foot

Will	|	Change key. Will not bigword you you don't barnyard me. Will wax no more. My songmoon no record wane mine not yours.
Shack	|	You see it out there I hear it in here sure. Leaf-listings fallen to frost-shimmy, sun gone cold, gone south. Gun-gray geese, those blood-drawn veerings that out-grace grace.

Ma	Always one woman keep drawin up buckets. Spill make stones darkshine, make mud mud. Rope water up. Big she bend strong back down. Wide feet, wide whatnot. Always water there, always all what needful, always enough.
Lovie	Need no slow ocean. Spill stream past, cold-over one. Froth up food for slim-slick trout. Down outloves level.
Nix	Not slick enough'll stop that. No spill today, nat means no spill never. Short sell hustle me undone. Shoulda held, shoulda held.
Countin'	Sugar maple, shadbush, sycamore, sassafrass, shagbark, rosa sharon.

Shake It

Nigger #2	Believe you then neither.
Sporting house	Hard-coded, what we're showin you is. Sing out, show out, hack access down three sold-over regionicities.
Papa mutt	Don't think so.
Grandpa's spells	Shouldna mowed no lawn, notnee's at old, notna sun's so hot. Shoulda stayed inside. Missed him he stepped out. Miss him plenty. Miss him still.
Mamanita	No more knock-kneed noise once we roll around. Call down carpet burn. Come on.
Pearls	Knot tween each mean only one roll off lost when the got-to get him hurry-up clumsy.
Crave	Circle the house while I sleep. Feel no need to speak. Like dark cold cloudshine. Know all what upwind.

Deep creek	Go slow. Deep creek call out all over, gather brown all falldown all riseup. Deep creek kiss river, give all over, level down to no bounds gone green water.

Emergency

Selma	Traded my weather for Deetroit weather. Cold snap come sometime I know, come some big snow. No point front porch, smoke smell outsell sweat. Sing inside, time come for me to.
Big	Omigod.
Downhearted	Took two T-shirts, done my ten days' time. Wash dishes all the yelled-at night, eat the leavins, you'd take T-shirts too.
Jailhouse	Had one window wouldn't mind. Nobody free miss me, but don't I miss that strong strong sun. New name some days, now song. Still Selma most. Sweet Selma.
Lost your head	Same time I lost mine. Lose it again next you.
City blues	Miss oakshade cool. Snow here make no mud. Miss bramblescars, tickitches. Miss mushrooms. Miss pickin burrs off socks. Miss meet me deershy in the clearing. Miss no cars no trains sweet owlcall sleep.
Darling	We woan do nothin you doan wanna.

I've Found a New Baby

Ja da	Everybody wanna see Paris once. Everybody love to learn a new song.
Logic	Follow south some attribute south of God grown big, grown nine-month big outta some twist headed north.

| Limehouse | | Modest place, that place we go. Course shade cover it cool. Course the browned-down pine quills quilt it soft. Course that spring still colds on up there. |

| Wild cat | | Stay too long mean not really there. Not there now musta never been. |

| Cake walkin' babies | | Sing barbershop, sing bow tie and striped shirt and straw, sing because. Because straw man strung down, strung out, strung together, because you know why I sing, why I stop. Because you *are* why. Sing down that striped shirt, sing off those soft shoes, that bass sweeping up slow those sweet lines that tenor left swift behind. |

| Shag | | Then dyin again to make sure. |

I Can Study Rain

| Delta | | Last year drop down clay this year spread out water. Start out snow way up there turn orchids here. |

| Twenty-nine songs | | Buckets from a well drilled down to hell. No, spills sloshed from buckets. No, mud made by spills. No, what seeps through mud all the way down. |

| Low-down achin' | | *She want fifty cents and I lacks a nickel.* |

| Me and the devil | | First deal I struck a real winner. You. That done down one mouth moment for all the rest. |

| Passway | | Two good eyes, but don't do dark. Don't do this tunnel under ash mountain. Seem long, seem real long, seem oughta be out now, oughta be light. Still walk, still cold, still down. No turnin back, just as dark behind. I hear her cryin, a ways back or a ways ahead. Can't tell. Two good ears, but hear the same thing all the time. Two good legs go forward just find more cold more wet. Light gone out |

long time back. This love note scrawled in the dark left for anybody crawl down this far got fingers good enough to feel what it whisper.

Hellhound | Kennel anything long enough it'll howl at whatever shows solo over where the whittled earth drops off.

Two stepfathers | And can't but one give you your name.

Hot-foot powder | Cut feet sore. Got loud, got cold, got hot, got salt. Need no more for dancin but you. Or what I still got, the thought of you.

Ramblin' | Places I been I ain't missed much but ain't seen no white squirrels like you got here.

Shines | One-line sun love this lake run one finger up her back mornin down again night.

Prelude to a Kiss

Bubber | Get down train some town you know nobody, nothin for when you walk but whistle.

Plug | Powder cap, carbon cushion, yellow-footed chanterelle, imperial cat, blood-red cort, pestle-shaped coral, cystoderma, corpse finder.

Aunt Tillie | Liked the phrase *vaguely sinful*, lived like they made it just for her.

Hot and sweet | What exactly could a lover write on those last postcards from the edge of the world? Why can only singing bring her back through expanding black? Is there no light but stars at the bounds of this blasted universe, calling back to our sad bright planet?

Chalumeau	What if I don't draw this landscape in a certain light at one moment from one station? What if instead of placing others in it I move through it myself? What if I see it as numbers, as sequence, as something that erases me, proof not that I was here but that I never existed, and could not possibly? What if I don't see this landscape at all, but hear it singing in my head, hear it sing swingingly?
Cootie	Sometime anger at the start, alway sorrow in the end.
Cup-muted	Later, baby. Not now. Not right now.
Blue serge	Dress up gone to see you.
Mood indigo	Love felt like falling asleep in snow, knowing, not choosing exactly but not resisting either, fascinated by this cold cold light bent blue.
Dusk	Why not love coming-on dark? Bats sing their way through this world.

Misbehavin'

Gully low	Maybe God speak shiny and smooth off mountains too, but my muddy Moses brung up rough scruff tablets from one brown down ditch. 1. Start small. 2. Meander. 3. Indiscriminate is good; grab anything that comes your way. 4. Carry it with you. 5. Carry it all with you. 6. Swell; flood. 7. Stop for no one. 8. Look back at mountains, forward to the sea. 9. Patience rubs rocks round; brown water washes white things clean. 10. Ascend and start over.
Sweet mama	First thing she did was laugh. I knew first thing.
Storyville	Trouble how much time you got when no one loves you.

Waifs	Can't find it on the streets don't need it.
Roseland	World I breathe need none better to back it up or come along after. Look pretty, smell good. It. You.
Lil	Diplodon, dosinia, donax, drupe, distorsio, drillia, dogwinkle, dwarf triton.
Gut bucket	Small disaster mean minor mercy.
Hotter than that	Less you can do about it, longer it takes to happen. First thing I saw, her eyes giving back light when she lifted her head. I knew she'd bolt, I knew I was going too fast, knew her fawn would follow. She could've gotten past, but it was like she stopped, like that was how she wanted both of us to die, her by my headlights, me by her body. Never mind I can tell you this. Doesn't mean she didn't get her wish.
Lyin' to myself	Can't sing what you can turn away from.

Sure Thing

Five by five	Followed you here. Why not? What else? Nothing not you matters now. Yes I knew better. No I won't go.
Tickle Joe	Don't stop followin my eyes just cause they lie, won't stop followin my fingers.
Doggin'	Scaphoid, lunate, triquetral, pisiform, trapezium, trapezoid, capitate, hamate, metacarpals, phalanges.
Small hotel	I had an interesting childhood, I know these things. So when she started bawling I knew to stack yesterday's colors against the ones before. She wanted to hurt herself, I know about these things. I had a colored

childhood. That's why they wear mascara, so you know they're crying. These things you learn after you hurt yourself, after they hurt you. I know a thing or two about stacking, about colors, about getting hurt, about the day before.

Stride | Left the bickering in the back room for the sure down shakin showin flesh out front. Sing no sad songs since.

Jumpin' | Happen when oughta-be-enough meet always-want-more.

'Way back | Starless night, dark deck, still sea, and they surfaced, those whales, like she sent them, spouting in sequence as if for that one moment she spoke through them before they dove again forever.

Cherry point | This one place we went to, being there made everything right. Night no darker there, stars no prettier, moon no bigger. No just-out-of-sight-waterfall sound silvered the air. We didn't talk more there. I didn't touch her. Didn't need to. Wanted nothing. Didn't gaze into her eyes. We didn't look at each other, just watched the world. Not that it came to us there, but that there—only there, only then—it had never gone away.

Swings the Band

Moonglow | *This* light.

Atlanta | The band was swingin and I only heard the gun in my one good ear.

Little Joe | Taught me a man lose his color he fall hard down.

Zodiac | Heard the whole thing, but my eyes never *did* adjust.

Black Christ	Which first pled *save me*, she or he, neither knew. *If I kilned you in clay I would glaze you black.* She said. Or he did. I am *black, and have been always, though only your molding me so showed me the fact.* He said. Or she did. Either way, either way.
Rose	How many loves can name themselves? How many cannot?
Elfrieda	Wunna you boys rough-burl me some elbowed walnut first, then somebody spindle me up some sabled maple.
Mass	You call God proper think he sit on benches straight think he don't slouch think he try to echo think he home all that cold stone. Meantime I be playin lessee he don't come dance.

These Foolish Things

Can't get started	It ain't speakin to me I ain't speakin back.
Strange fruit	Didn't pass by many sins, wasn't gonna not taste you.
Funny that way	Wore-out run-down-to-mud same-way-every-time-I-let-her-out got-no-kinda-sense one-corner-to-another-then-all-around-the-fence nose-down-like-she-could-catch-a-rabbit-anyway kind of path.
Drinkard	Falling-loud fountain's steady-hush sound.
Tenderly	Him bein that old make me what? When he was a baby I rocked that boy a many a mile.
All of me	Can't give you what I never had myself.
44	Come between me and you. Like everything else now. Telephone. Time zone. Feeble neighbors' lawns, overgrown. Get in line, 44, get in line.

Stormy weather	I told em wash her no more, her skin so thin. Walked back in she was bleedin, washed her skin right off.
Gotta right	To tell myself the truth while I lie to you. Gotta right to *try* to hear the snow. Gotta right to wake up for sounds you can't hear, then be fraid to fall back to sleep. Gotta right to first-dime whisky, second-dime bread. Gotta right to prefer after to before. To hoard alibis. To end with nothin if I started that way.

Palisades

Dizzy	Snow fuss a halo of the light, or light a halo of the snow?
Cheraw	Aspen she grow, more root than branch, earth-burrowed soul even when she shivers back the sun, one in all her risings, movin under me many so seasons surround me now.
Shaw 'nuff	Them things shaw 'nuff purty. Touch em? Hold em? Gentle I be. Real gentle.
Quilombo	First field verify floating walls then reclaim flexible space. Six throws of the hand shut it all down. Lose power to the core the code locks, three thousand kelvin knuckle and all. Fifty seats, static, find four floral columns staged to monitor a tricky world.
Nana	Can sing it it's one of my names, can't it's one of yours.
Siboney	In my dream you still loved me. In my dream it had been true once that you did love me, not only that I wanted you to, so it was possible for you to love me still, or at least possible for you to love me still despite your not having loved me before. Such is the logic of sleep, a logic I swallowed in my efforts to survive waking life. A bundle

of wires insulated in bright colors, coiled into a sort of sleeve, sent off sparks when I put my arm in it. I think. Some parts of the dream felt uncertain, but that love was possible I remember clearly, so remarkable it seemed.

Caribe | Try to name what I want, I see you, I say this.

Well You Needn't

Round midnight | This dark she open the door light come in or go out?

Chaser | Small glass splinter look like a tiny fuse in my right index finger, pull it out not cause it hurt but to show off.

Epistrophy | Three minutes here, three minutes there, three take a life, three give one back, three minutes find a new baby, three minutes tell why, three say nothin don't need to, three minutes hang on, three let go, three minutes your eyes close your arms around me sway, three minutes touch my wrist look in my eyes, three got to, three don't, three minutes always starting always done.

Misterioso | Somethin in me say same deflections left me outta your world showed me one of my own. Somethin in me say everything sing, say listen. Somethin in me say God work off by himself sometimes, don't say much. Somethin in me say stay home a year, nothin to hear can't hear in my head.

Bemsha | Flexor pollicis brevis, abductor digiti minimi, lumbrical, annular pulleys, cruciate pulleys.

Evidence | The answer. You are. That I am here. To my existence. On this planet. Whose sun. Though I am alone. When it explodes. I am here. Here night shimmers in the north. Answer. Me.

| I mean you | Came right up in the yard they did, quiet as you please, six of em together. I was working on the shutters had my back to em didn't know they were there till I heard em chewing. Come for fallen fruit under the pear tree they had. I shifted on the ladder just a little, and they all looked up together with those big dark eyes like they were all one animal but then they just went back to eating. I watched em and thought they'd stay longer but they walked off quick as they came like they knew I'd see nothin so beautiful ever again. |

Melancholy Me

| Scat | On the end got a hook some words do, ain't sense they seek. Down they go fishin in you find your swimmin-dumb soul. |

| Coloratura | Scalloped sootywing, california sister, ruby-spotted swallowtail, pink-edged sulphur, carolina satyr, sickle-winged skipper, sachem. |

| Intervallic | Take nothin with you, bring nothin back. |

| Not for me | Not a nightmare if it tells me what I didn't know. |

| Early autumn | Fine gold this first bright cold foisted on these half-buried bones. White soon but not now, these knobs, knuckles, knees. Not white quite yet, this crooked spine. |

| Soon | Cattails in shallow water, one tree tall among em. |

Say When

| Swingmatism | You hear a *bird* sing, you don't try to understand. |

| Sissle | Listen to anything long enough it'll tell you your life. |

Tiny	|	Pine siskin, dickcissel, longspur, purple finch, lark sparrow, wheatear, winter wren, waterthrush, veery.
Ornithology	|	Bird dream felt like fell from the nest, felt like gray and wet, felt like big eyes never opened. Useless yellow beak. No cat, sure, but crows and ants and which is worse? Done nothin wrong don't matter. Felt like grass hide me but not long. Felt like fell this once never gonna fly.
How high the moon	|	She sparrow. He owl.
Klacktoveedsedstene	|	Keep flyin low over my head, them birds. I reach up finally and touch one passin by. Touch it, touch her.
Heroin	|	Start out skitter of swifts, end up leaf trapped in a sheeta ice.
Confirmation	|	Spectin me to answer or spectin me to sing?

Black Coffee

Desire	|	Somebody gotta ask why not.
This mood	|	Lay down step down rock trickle moss-quiet creek come down two wet-hush hollows meet steady down fern-green downy-back leaf-rustle keep cold brier-safe mudbreasted bluebird deer-drinkin shade.
Shulie	|	Baneberry, brickelbush, bear grass, mission bells, bitterroot, bleeding heart.
All I need	|	Mmm hm. Mmmm hm.
Mean to me	|	You is awful. You got no idea how much you.
It never	|	Seem like songs all say I died fore I was born. Seem like singin make me happiern you.

Now's the Time

Three deuces	What's the smallest space in which I can live my life whole?
Shh	Drowned city dreamed long enough'll wave you green and quiet and slick. Shopping carts curled off boats by beered-up boys cold to a lattice of rust. Bubble-nuzzled, scale-fondled, fin-skimmed. Last past how you know to live.
Sly	How birds pass through pickets on a bare-wood fence: land feet-first on the lower rail, then lean forward to take off on the other side.
So what	My *life* is forbidden.
Nefertiti	Carry you with me. Yes you is. Yes I do.
Zouk	The way a tree sounds in wind at the edge of the world.
Boplicity	Lives of passion and scrape.
Alton	Squirrels here fraid nobody but nervous now must be comin some kinda snow.

Sheets of Sound

Kolax	Some sensation sent up sell down data.
Montuna	Mountains rise out of song toward the god they intuit.
Cleanhead	Fall down showed me shouldna.
Whole tone	Black witch, wounded hawk, webworm, royal walnut, whistling, welsh wave, wainscot, pretty widow.
Trinkle	Softer than before sing warm through me wind.

A love supreme		Truth is I am nothing. Truth is too I could not make myself so, or see myself so by myself. I needed *it*, my nothingness. Now I hear.
Ascension		Cold train go slow uphill through snow. Slow uphill anyway. Wide bed fold up into wall. Ladder lean against.
Pursuance		If I believed I'd've tried to say plain what I said crooked. If I believed I'd've said what I sung.

THE WELL-TEMPERED CLAVIER

Prelude and Fugue No. 1 in C

My life makes sense the way a wildebeest's does: first weakened by illness and thirst:
then separated from the herd then surrounded then captured: one lioness takes his
neck in her jaws: the others have his hindquarters: dust rises and the brittle grasses
give way goodbye goodbye: the beast's eyes bloom with fear and ecstasy: first he
knows nothing then he feels nothing: finally his front legs buckle.

•

disbelief won't stop our speaking to you
don't wait for us to say who we are
that's the least of your worries
listen for names you might hear poison
settle at night on the grass
soak through the pads in your dog's paws
disbelief won't stop our falling in love
everything here is like everything there
except there light reflects off faces
here light shines all the way through us
there dusk has begun coming earlier
here dusk always comes earlier
disbelief won't stop our telling you lies
don't wait for love to return
it never comes back it follows us
listen for names you might hear yours
in the fog muted and diffuse
fog the atmosphere most like us
disbelief won't stop our betraying you
is that thunder we want rain
rain the weather most like us
here we fall in love again and again
roses still die back to black stalk here
that it can't be never stopped love before

we fall in love here trust us trust us
our faces die back their petals brown
and fall to the poisoned grass
it's always getting dark here
always dusk the light most like us

Prelude and Fugue No. 2 in C Minor

My cold cold salty desire: schools of krill spilled silver from light to light: whales
jailing krill in bubbles before bursting on them from below: invisible algae and
plankton suffusing the whole: seaweed waving goodbye goodbye: jellyfish these
floating moons morsing your name here where it cannot be spoken: sperm whale
fighting squid to the death far below any light: penguins sliding off ice into might
as well be: elephant seals swimming deeper than radio signals can sink goodbye
goodbye: orcas close to ice cruising for antarctic cod: cephalopods signaling
complex codes of color and gesture: crinoids fanning for algae in eerie light beneath
the ice: swollen tubeworms swaying over volcanic vents: luminous fish as far below
day as stars stay above it: orcas bobbing up to peer across the ice then sending
signals with their intricate exhalations.

•

he asked me and I said no which was a half-truth
half a truth was all I had all love left me
I am myself a half-truth now whatever I was before
whatever I was back then when I thought I never lied
before I learned I always had lied to him and to myself
before I learned love itself is hardly half a truth
before I learned there are no whole truths
nothing that guileful god flaw has not fondled
of our ascertainings our words our bodies
before I knew I didn't *want* the truth
not because I couldn't bear it I can't bear what I am now
but because the me who thought she was telling the truth
also thought she could be satisfied
and this me can't bear the half-self love left me
after it asked me what it asked and I said no

Prelude and Fugue No. 3 in C-sharp

I lived half a life: I knew before it ended it would end this way less malice or meaning: this pair of errant headlights bearing down: exactly half a life: I knew I would see its end coming: picking up speed aiming at me: half a life in all the ways one might mean that: the other driver too drunk to choose worn lane stripes over temptation: two bright eyes inviting this consuming kiss: at the moment of the wreck folding metal told me God was her lover: who else could make my inner life so counter to my outer: who else would throw me away while he was claiming her: who else could tire of swans and showers of gold and burning bushes: who else could come as cancer to claim her from the inside out.

•

we are consuming you because we can because we must
we started with your breasts because he loved them so
we started there to prove we loved them even more
but then we had to prove we loved all of you
as much as he loved your every part and aspect
and after that we had to prove we loved only you
prove that needing nothing else we could become you
if only we could keep ourselves secret
until we were you and you us
we are consuming you because we can because we must
because it is our nature to consume and yours to be consumed
because we love you more than he does
because we love you more than anyone else could
because as love in its purest form we give you your purest form
we are consuming you because we can because we must
unlike his our need for you is absolute our hunger unmitigated
he loves you and himself and other women other objects other dreams
our affections are undivided so we ourselves divide
suppose we stopped what then
we would only prove we were lying to you and to ourselves
we had to continue we have to continue
until no distinction remains between our will and yours

between your body and ours your life and ours
we are consuming you because we can because we must
we are consuming you faster than lies are consuming him
dividing faster than the will divides for fear and hunger

Prelude and Fugue No. 4 in C-sharp Minor

My drifting desire: continents longing for the larger selves they lost long ago:
moonlust and salt that splits them still and will until rain finally wins its test of
will against rock: matching shorelines floating slowly apart goodbye goodbye:
hissing lava weeping at the seams: earthquakes sighing over slow slow slow
separation: rift valleys gathering their inhospitable pools: flamingoes phoenixed
from the scalding waters.

                    •

if you were going to you should not have waited so long
if you were going to you should have planned it
or planned it better don't lie to yourself you *did* plan it
if you were going to you should have more than once
you should be now why are you listening to us
if you wanted a secret life you should have kept it secret
or made it a life you soulless bastard
escape now into your body this is your last chance
don't add this to your list of failures
it will be the grain that pushes you under
the dead speak only to those who might as well be
we are helpless before our desires for ourselves
but we can make our desires for *you* come true
and they may not match your own desires
we will keep talking though not to you for long
because she will be gone and you will be with us
giving up again and again all the gifts
you always knew the universe would take back
including her especially her

Prelude and Fugue No. 5 in D

Everything turned to music in my head: my fingers followed but not fast enough:
I had no talent but I was possessed: for one moment I gave up all I had: nothing
and the illusion it was love: everything turned to music in my head: music doesn't
have to live here in the world: God might sell music but he doesn't give: I had no
talent I was just possessed: I saw what I doubt so often repeated I had to *insist* on
disbelief: everything turned to music in my head: what God promised me and what
he threatened looked alike after you took your blouse off: though I had no talent I
was possessed: nothing ever *just happens* but you did: had you not killed me I would
have killed myself: everything turned to music in my head: I had no talent but I
was possessed.

⋅

I am the angel of buckled steel
I am the angel of long blank scratchy messages
angel of the concluding click and dial tone
of qualities of character you admire but do not possess
I am the angel of diplomacy undone
angel of surreptitious longings all longings *are* surreptitious
I am the tap and knock of cooling metal
star-bright eyes watching from the woods
crushed milk cartons cross-shredded documents
another nerve center burned beyond recall
I am your almost lover your many lovers never to be
though God himself can't name them all
all those fugitive desert flowers dormant between rains
I am the angel of all your corrupt inclinations
and just so you'll know you will try and try the rest of your life
but you can never make her happy though you can make her sad
every decision you make will prove worse than the last
original sin needs no god and you are the proof

Prelude and Fugue No. 6 in D Minor

My clandestine desire: seated woman in a lit room seen from the street releasing her
hair from a french braid and brushing it smooth with slow slow strokes: her steam-
heated second-floor room: how her hair alters the name *auburn*: the tiny sparks her
brush strokes coax that would be visible were the watcher with her and the room
dark: the sound of her brush separating the strands goodbye goodbye: steam fighting
the pipes for release: her bare shoulders changing shape through each stroke: the
longing with which she looks into her own dark eyes.

    •

the gods keep to themselves even here especially here
we hear them yes but in whispers inscrutably
like voices in another room less heard than intuited
the gods keep to themselves everywhere
their mumbling indistinct between gusts of wind
sometimes the living are spirits too
they speak in flashes of light we see them from the corners of our eyes
there are no souls here but there are voices
some nights the crickets make sense
sometimes even insects are spirits
don't try to name this voice don't try to locate it
the answer to all your questions about it is yes
is it from your wife yes is it from her lover yes
is it from your own bad conscience yes
is it from God yes of course the devil yes the devil too
is it from the dead yes from the boy you once picked a fight with yes
the first girl you loved yes the first you betrayed yes was she the same of course
from those who trusted you yes those who knew better yes
from the part of you that knew every piece of this long ago yes yes

Prelude and Fugue No. 7 in E-flat

When God took back her world the instant felt like falling backward into water:
above me bubbles sizzled into light: my feet and fingers flailed for fundament:

my senses flooded with fugitive clarity: had you not been so sudden and death so
sensuous I might have made more effort to swim: I thought I needed air until I left it.

　　•

we are less afraid than you are because our fears have been confirmed
you think we will give you advice you think we care about you
we neither love by your logic nor are bound by your body
we know why you want to sleep but also why you can't
the stairs and floorboards speak with your weight we speak with your dying
fear visits when you are dreaming and when are you not
we are less afraid than you are because our fears have been confirmed
we suffer here you will too what could stop that nothing nothing
we neither love by your logic nor are bound by your body
our voices know you as bodies to your souls so words to ours
the stairs and floorboards speak with your weight we speak with your dying
go on keep trying to sleep it would only prove you are us
we worry less than you do because our fears have been confirmed

Prelude and Fugue No. 8 in E-flat Minor

My white and ivory desire: a sheet of snow sliding slowly off a sloped roof goodbye
goodbye: origami swan swimming a lake of lace: rice on porcelain: snow as it slips
from the eave assuming the curve of your hips: that spring day sitting in bright sun
on stone stairs: what I know how to say to you sinking under what I don't: snow
landing on snow with a soft *oof.*

　　•

always and only of you
when I said God I meant you
when I said death I meant you
when I said your name
when I said someone else's
when I said nothing
when I said what you wanted to hear
or what you did not
when I insisted on what you had tried to deny

and admitted what I had tried to deny
when I told you the truth
when I told you lies which I did more often
when I told you something you could believe
when I told you something you couldn't
when I told you something you had to
though it was false and both of us knew it
and now my love especially now

Prelude and Fugue No. 9 in E

What I want has nothing to do with how I act: how I act has nothing to do with who I am: who I am has nothing to do with what I want: what I want haunts me an angry juvenile ghost: invisible destructive running through the rooms: what I want has nothing to do with how I act: I want a lot that I will never tell about: acts and people most of whom you know by name: who I am has nothing to do with what I want: my first death found my second when she and I met: their single shadow our substitute for time: what I want has nothing to do with how I act: my desires drink and pick fights and stay out all night: I sip tea and practice the piano at home: who I am has nothing to do with what I want: if only my happiness were not infinite: if only I had some respite from the sublime: that I want you I attic off from how I act: who I am I cellar away from what I want.

•

life proved less important than I thought
though also more beautiful far more beautiful
it hurts me less than I thought it would
to have no life no touching only voices
but it grieves me more if I could weep I would
I miss tear ducts I didn't use them enough
I miss my body I didn't use it often enough
I miss my lungs how they burned during runs on cold mornings
I miss my fingers they touched far too few hot beach rocks
and far too few tautly tendoned wrists of lovers

Prelude and Fugue No. 10 in E Minor

My sunburned desire: atop hot boulders lizards lying lazily across each other:
their pineal eyes that learned a hundred million years ago to track the sun: octopi
in shallow water hiding under rocks: bright quick colors caressing the fragile reef:
sand wearing itself smooth: the long long yawns of iguanas lolling leather tongues:
shorebirds fascinated by their intermittently submerged feet: pelicans diving and
diving: gulls in flight dropping shellfish onto rocks to break them open.

•

can a passacaglia be sung I can't remember
how does a tongue feel on the back of my neck I can't remember
or fingers tracing my shoulderblades I can't remember
who is speaking here me or her or you I don't remember
does love start because it has already started it must
did I fall in love with you because I was in love already I must have
has anything harmed me more than love no nothing
how does it feel to meet another's eyes and be unable to breathe I can't remember
what is it like to hear your lover's voice *and* touch her body I can't remember
though I can still name what I miss about the old life
hiss of water in pipes the curve of a particular spine
breaking up clods of clay to mix them with peat
squirrels hanging by their back paws stretching down
to clutch clusters of maple seeds at the ends of branches
pairs of maple seeds shaped like bats handfuls of spent flowers
I miss holding a steaming cup of tea while standing in snow
I miss hummingbirds hummingbirds above all hummingbirds
anything that feeds on flowers and shines in the sun
and need not sing because it can fly backward
knows something gods would keep to themselves if there were gods

Prelude and Fugue No. 11 in F

Had we not kissed cartographers would not have mapped the mud nor species
diverged nor continents floated apart: had we not kissed we would never have been
born: nor our ancestors crossed the savannah through chest-high grass on their

two new legs or left the hunt-stained caves goodbye goodbye: flowers would not have beckoned bees nor trees risen from clay nor their leaves fallen back to form fossils: nor planets wandered nor galaxies formed nor stars burned out nor nebulae spawned lavender clouds larger than any possible human world though no larger than our impossible one.

•

I always heard voices I thought everyone did
I can't tell you what I'm crying about though it will kill you too
the voice of the real comes from a ghost that's the problem
if I spent less time naming my cravings at night
or knew fewer cravings to name
I might be speaking now through someone else
bringing better news and to more people
the voice of the real comes from a ghost that's the problem
the unspared can speak to the spared
but the spared cannot speak back
the voice of the real comes from a ghost that's the problem
this is my only voice you only listen when I'm sleeping
when you think you're hearing someone else
the voice of the real comes from a ghost that's the problem
the real cannot speak but the rest can and does
which means if you can speak you are not real
and it means I break the rule

Prelude and Fugue No. 12 in F Minor

My parched desire: the way nomads at a drying water hole in Mali wait for the elephants to leave: how the herd knows when to start across the desert goodbye goodbye: their urge for the savannah on the other side: relentless desert sun: the number who will die during migration: lives lived from water to water and ended in between: how the dead will be consumed and by what voracious patiences: that the others will continue: how they know when the rains will come: that they know what will be green beyond the sandstone ridge: how the whole herd learned what no one elephant knows.

•

call it somaphagia we are eating your sleep
a sweet to make any devils envy us
you wouldn't listen until we started eating you
then it was too late at first we were just warning you
then we loved you and nothing is more deadly
you wouldn't listen so we started eating you
we knew before you held her hand you were going to
we knew how long that first kiss would last
we saw it before you did we know what you don't know
and never will about her and about yourself
you didn't listen when we started eating you
you thought you knew yourself everyone thinks that
but the person you knew was not you and never had been
keep trying not to listen but we have started eating you
we heard what you told her yesterday
we know what you will tell her tomorrow
we know why she believes you though she knows you are lying
and why you think you are telling the truth when you lie to her
and how long it would take her to stop believing you
if you were going to live that long
don't listen then but now that we are eating you
we know how soon you will stop believing yourself

Prelude and Fugue No. 13 in F-sharp

She knew before I knew: it was she who told me: she held my heart in her two
hands and read it: my heart blue and packed in ice and very still: her cordomancy
told her and I listened at night while the voices that ate her ate her alive: in twenty-
four keys she spoke in her sleep: with forty-eight fires Bach invented the sun: with
forty-eight outlines Shostakovich tried to trace his own uncertain but certainly
shadowed shadow: twenty-four nights she spoke in her sleep or *he* spoke or *they*
did the voices whoever they were: I only had to cradle her head the way she cradles
hearts and they spoke: all you do she said is turn it this way turn it that when the
doctors say: focus on holding still so they can sew: she said only holding someone
else's failing heart helped her feel her own: *they* said nothing I did not know: they

said she would die: they said I would die: they told me when and how: in twenty-four fugues they said goodbye goodbye: find here so many preludes more for the trunk of my car: I wanted to see if these two dozen would burn: I knew I would: I knew I already had.

> •

I substituted love when denied happiness
I substituted loyalty when love withdrew
I substituted pretense because I had been disloyal
long ago from the start always
I substituted sullenness when I failed at pretense
I settled in the end on self-destruction
something I know now I have a talent for
I know my name only when I see it
spelled on your irises in a code no one else knows
I know your name when I speak it the only way I can
stroking your neck with my thumb
I leave with you the name I need no longer
spelled on a yellow ginkgo leaf

Prelude and Fugue No. 14 in F-sharp Minor

My alien desire: brown broadened to green in a river delta seen from above: salt replacing surrendered silt: barracuda in place of piranha: ancestors buried in biers up the sides of cliffs: children buried in the trunks of trees to be carried to heaven by their growth: birdhouse-sized shrines built for small furtive saints and hung in trees: infant sea turtles' ungainly race across moonlit sand: the first turtle's feeling as a withdrawing wave lifts it into the sea: adult turtles' ghostly floating goodbye goodbye: one eel curled in an s mouth open motionless on brown sand and dead coral: inland an underground river flowing through karst: waves breaking over and over on towered lava their white foam patiently shaping its stacked black sheets.

> •

why curse desire when you must breathe it
why be content with a single voice
who would we love if not for ghosts
how will you know the lies we tell from the truths

how will you distinguish lies you want to believe from ones you should
will you trust the voices from nowhere enough to follow their commands
if so why if not why not
who would we love if not for ghosts
why are we speaking to you and why were you listening for us so late
why were you still awake why are you awake now
why would we *want* to understand our own words
why would our saying them make them ours
who would we love if not for ghosts
do you trust your urges your instincts your memory
do you trust your judgment do you trust the voices in your head
can you still trust what you know is leading you to death
can you follow what you distrust in preference to what you trust
or maybe we should ask that the other way around
who would we love if not for ghosts
what are you listening for how will you know when you hear it
do the voices come from her dreams or our dreams or yours
what would you tell us if you knew anything
what do you wish you could tell that you can't
who do you wish you could tell it to
who would we love if not for ghosts
why is it forbidden to love more than one person
give us a good answer to *that*

Prelude and Fugue No. 15 in G

A kiss may be demonic or divine or both at once like a familiar song: a kiss can end
your life one ended mine: now I understand original sin: no one but you ever *was*
listening: a kiss may be demonic or divine: my affections are strong my actions
mean: I did what I did instead of thinking: a kiss can change your life one altered
mine: wings folded my desires sleep upside down then swarm out at dusk and see
by singing: a kiss may be demonic or divine: a butterfly warming itself in bright sun
can light on your hand and pulse its wings: a kiss can end your life one ended mine:
why would I live any moment again if the first time was not devastating: a kiss may
be demonic or divine: the kiss that gave me your life ended mine.

•

we were happier when you let me decide what lies to tell you
instead of demanding lies you thought you wanted to hear
I was never who either of us thought I was
is it love to lie and tell you so or to lie and say I'm not
in the end *everything* gets left out of the story
if I had told better lies I might have believed myself
if this answers questions they are not the ones I asked
and certainly not the ones you think I should answer
the living ask different questions than the dead answer
we might have made it if you had let me lie
I might have told better lies if I had believed myself
I might still love you if you had let me not know for sure
we were happier when you let me lie to myself
decide now how honest you want me to be and about what

Prelude and Fugue No. 16 in G Minor

My silver gelatin desire: arms raised praising the naked name of napalm: a bare-
shouldered man whose own biceps make him bow: corn-stubble bowing to vacant
house and vacant horizon: backs leaving a landing boat leaning forward waist-high
in waves: schools of bullets swimming swiftly by: ten white body bags fugitive
into the sea: two white grocery bags steadfast in front of a tank: one pacific body
engulfed in its own flames.

•

sometimes we doubt your existence too
we speak with or without your listening
we keep talking what else can we do
maybe you need us worse than we need you
maybe you are no more real than we are
we sometimes doubt your existence too
you want us in your mouth to chew
but we are voices only voices
we keep talking what else can we do
if you weren't there our words would put you there
what shows you otherwise maybe they do

we sometimes doubt your existence too
to us *you* are only voices
you think they only overwhelm you
but we still feel memory and desire
these words these words are all we know to do

Prelude and Fugue No. 17 in A-flat

What I think when I try not to think of you: I think of Bach in place of your bare belly: I think of the meteor shower to remember that things burning out bring joy: of the middle term between desire and death *that* is what I seek: I think I washed up on shore and stand before you naked and dirty speaking in lieu of clasping your knees: I think the heat this time of year rises to mimic the gradual lifting away of my life: I think only the disembodied speak only the disembodied listen: I think elements more crucial than air surround and inhabit me: I think the first seven victims of the world fell to your hands and three or four of them were me: if souls could suffocate mine would have long ago: and souls *can* suffocate and mine did: I think another lost son struggles home hungry and ashamed: his inheritance was not enough his name is me: I think the truth is murderous and bent on killing *me*: I left my lesson early I think you were my teacher goodbye goodbye: I think the gods created everything but orchids which fallen angels make as gifts for one another: I think I was better off before I knew what I was missing.

•

I meant what I implied by saying what I said
and doing what I did after what you did
after you said what you promised you would never say
I meant you should listen with your wrists
I meant *I* should listen with your wrists
I meant you are bright light I am shattered glass
happy to be fractured if the pieces shine
I meant both of us know enough to name
the hummingbird in your feathered hand

Prelude and Fugue No. 18 in G-sharp Minor

My ancient desire: captured from an asteroid matter older than our solar system: the constant background craving-naming of the crows interrupted by the intermittent givings-up of geese: twisted bristlecone pine clinging to a ledge: the ledge leaning into wind: rhizome the size of a sea that was under the first mammal's foot: hardwood kelson hosting coral.

•

you are the price of my restlessness and I am willing to pay
you made my life a life left behind
your shoulders your shoulders your knees your neck
your lips o jesus your lips the mole on your back your neck
your hands and fingers your ankles your eyes your neck
twenty years of sleep for twenty minutes of waking
and I would trade again I refuse to disown my desire
I left home knowing my judgment was impaired
knowing I loved you more than you loved me
knowing I loved you more than I valued my happiness
it could not have been me your arms were speaking to
but I listened and I heard what I wanted to hear
I wanted to hear what spoke through your arms
when it said truths too arrange themselves in constellations
my love for you *is* my will to death
because of you everyone after you no one
I sing of you because you stand for all I cannot sing
I can call to you I still do I will call to you always
from here from one small impossibility away
the sound of your voice is enough
it has to be nothing else is left me to hold
I hear you in the plants I smell you in the thunder
what I don't believe haunts me who I can't hold haunts me
what I held when I held you was more than you it was the spirits
what held you when I held you was more than me
it was the spirits it was all their songs

Prelude and Fugue No. 19 in A

I remember every kiss until I fell in love: the list of all I have includes nothing I
desire: one kiss I take with me where it sent me to my grave: my desires fit my life
like a second right-hand glove: the soul generates light only at its departure:
I remember every kiss until I fell in love: once I wanted happiness I *wanted* to
believe: now I find I much prefer the solace of despair: the kiss I carry with me I
carry to my grave: anything intense enough to feel is fugitive: nothing I want lasts
long enough to name or declare: I remembered every kiss after I fell in love: you
are my failure to conceal everything I crave: till you showed me I didn't know I
was what we are: the kiss no one can take away sent me to my grave: even if I *could*
remain intact I wouldn't have: I had looked for myself before and found nothing
there: I remember every kiss as your one kiss my love: the one kiss I carry with me
still here in my grave.

•

yes to all your questions yes to those you do not ask
yes no matter what the answer ought to be
yes I love you yes of course no not more than I love her
yes you can love two people but one won't want to know
yes there are laws but no one tells us either
yes I stopped speaking your name out loud
no I did not stop *repeating* your name
I can't keep it secret so I say it to myself
yes love becomes infinite distance and endlessly repeating your name
yes you made me suffer then yes I suffer still
yes I want to suffer more if it means you

Prelude and Fugue No. 20 in A Minor

My winter-dented desire: blacktop laid down too near the shore broken off the road
in chunks: the same sunken road seen through leaning trees: rain-dark mulch pock-
marked where squirrels dug up bulbs: hollow places creatures find to hibernate: the
flowered places far away to which they fly: wet leaves under snow hosting mold:
lone leaf caught in a cobweb between a window and its shutter.

•

I know what you want I had your desires
I *became* your desires that is my hell
you want another life more lives
with more lovers and you will get those lives
you are getting them now without knowing it
more lives all as empty and unknowing as this one
all as drained by unfulfilled desire
each beautiful and generous lover
shadowed by another you cannot have
you may love as much as you want
but have none of what you love
first I sank in water then I sank in light

Prelude and Fugue No. 21 in B-flat

I cannot see you from here: I can draw no closer but love I smell you still: I kiss you
in the only way I can: the way we kiss who cannot kiss: who bloom but briefly: who
make as make we must bright fertile colors of our muddy yearnings: I kiss you with
sheer wings and six pollen-laden legs: I send you another bee.

•

time here is a function of the voice
here your voice is not *your* voice
sleep is a function of the voice
sleep itself speaks until others speak through it
your voice here is a function of the spirit
it is not *you* anymore afterward not anyone
we are no one in particular certainly not you
we are inseparable indistinguishable
we are your lover and your husband alike
we do not distinguish as you do
even between the dead and the living
so we speak to you from beyond
but we are also of those
who are not yet beyond as you see things
though you will see as we see soon enough

Prelude and Fugue No. 22 in B-flat Minor

My saurian desire: sensory cells that dot my jaw and detect even tiny vibrations: a valve at the back of my throat to keep out water: mirrors behind my eyes to double light at night: my urge to carry my young in my mouth to the water after they hatch: the ability to hold my breath underwater and lie motionless for hours at the bottom waiting for prey: my tiny tiny brain that knows only hunger but knows it well: the months one meal can last me: my instinct to roll so that I twist off whatever limb my jaws have clutched: the 240 million years that make mine the oldest hunger.

•

when I die let them find me in your arms
when your arms found me I was dying already
I started dying when I became yours
in your arms I died again and again
I was yours long before you found me
when I die let them find me in your arms
I speak to you now that I am dead
from the beginning your arms spoke to me
I started dying when I became yours
I answered one death with another
I taste you still though I no longer see
when I die let them find me in your arms
now in my death I speak of your arms
if I die in your arms let no one find me
I started dying when I became yours
you found me because I was dying
I became yours because I was dying
when I die let them find me in your arms
I started dying when I became yours

Prelude and Fugue No. 23 in B

After the crash I plan to be the god of symmetry and silhouette: of the light bright behind you: of dusk on the hill behind another mona lisa: of the scurfed skin on a turtle's neck: after the wreck I aim to be the god who makes your irises who sets in those two circles six hundred glacial lakes seen from the sky: after the crash after I can no longer listen let someone else: I plan at last to have a voice of my own in the next world a brighter world than this one but still made of clay.

•

we are voices it is our work to send you careening
from consciousness to consciousness like tumbling down a hill
voices need neither motive nor cause
one thing following from another is your idea not ours
we speak and you insist on moving your lips
naming all we have given up will take us forever
bring bundles bring baskets bowls we are hungry
how will you know which of our night visits is the last
do you want to know or would it be better not to
we speak like bleeding you go pale
and have to find a way to stop it or you die
your body *is* your soul it *will* die
we are not souls we are voices
nothing else is left us but our hunger
you think hunger comes from your body
that at least you will be released from it when you die
but hunger will remain always it is your voice
it's not that we're damned no one is damned
but some lose their voice and others never had one
because we speak through someone asleep
you wonder if we tell the truth
but why not take it as a sign that we do

Prelude and Fugue No. 24 in B Minor

Had I lived my cursive would have reverted to print: my capitals to lower case: had I lived she would have left me: she always liked me better dead: had I lived the river would have taken longer to find its fated sea: had the swollen creek I thought I could cross not swept me away I might have seen the doe in her seclusion giving birth: I might have stood in the woods and heard the breeze advancing tree by tree: had the horse I thought I could break not thrown me I might have made it across the plains: I might not have been caught by the grass fires: had the squall not surprised me so far from shore I might have watched the waves from safety instead of sinking under them: as it is the depth of the blue here compensates for the pressure and the cold.

•

love you or inhabit you you know which one I chose
I still count it secret if I say it only to the living
I believed everything except the voices now I am one
I who feared voices from another world became what I feared
I regret that I did not know sooner you wanted to destroy your life
as badly as I wanted to destroy mine
and you wanted *me* to destroy it I would have tried
you should have ruined me half a life ago
maybe I knew you then maybe you destroyed my life before it began
I regret my past virtues I renounce them all though now it is too late
now I think always and only of my vices
you were one and I want more
I did not speak until you started listening
the others speak all the time but I have been waiting for you
speaking only to speak your name
your name that I say over and over
your name that I carry your name that carries me

ALL THE ONE-EYED BOYS IN TOWN

to flatten your portrait of God, to make it plain,
why not confess to restless
rivulets? **Breezes sing** in
coded sequence, the path loves
the forest or pities it,
when earth crusts forth oracle
my fears echo as your voice.
All oaks mimic this oak: black,
unsatisfactory as
love, worn down more by each rain.
It doesn't matter, the world.
No one saw room in my guilt
for your lush, wild elegance.
It's like watching a movie of reasoning, this

incomplete explanation, this relationship
breathing your body over
all nine of my fingertips.
Like rain improvising, I
traced **the song of sufficient
reason** down your spine. Swallows
stopped circling, but my terror
proves those cold swift streams we ran
were not rivers at all. Not
musician enough to stunt
the grammatical, I'm left
listening for lost moments,
their improbabilities
of sequence imposing episodes between you

and what shines. Only after my tongue was cut out
could I ride my nightmare through

garden-given gaspings, seeds
sinking through seawater, one
death to another. **Tell me**
what this means, our fall, your tongue
and clitoris, swollen with
something halted, wrong acres
brailled with a wisping of down.
Did someone spill this sequence,
these petals flustered to earth?
Gods ignite themselves like snow.
I desire you, every seam
and flounce of you, sentenced into the languages

I speak out of my sleep, having dreamed them whole. I'll
let you cry. I've cried too much.
The heart ajar, born wounded,
buys its crusts with begged-for coins.
Sequence hums, asserts again
the soul is shared. An atoll,
its little sunken island.
She bled doubt out. He stole through
one world but not her others.
It's hot, yes, but we're not here
for long, suffocated by
such exquisite reds, yellows,
greens, so marginal and frail.
We locked the doors—remember?—and let our lovers

become less real, less urgent, less moonscarred and gnarled.
But what sings from water-clear,
sequenced, sufficient wonder,
cigarette smoke, spent tea bags,
a never-was-golden day,
will cover all our losses:

those five-dollar-a-week rooms,
no one to name us, to risk
the breath train from Leningrad,
swans **unmaking a willow**
by the river, women in
succulent undergarments,
past love but not love poems.
Everywhere you've hovered before, I meant to stand

while lights went out in the valley below. So what
if bright-bellied winter stars
nap overhead? The body
insinuates this: ashes
defining diaspora,
others' wars floodlit, crimson
confessions, wine-hued dreams that
tint dispassionate linens,
turn back the curved listless world
that sequences what I know,
notes you meant not to be heard.
Touch me, but if not your breath
will do, equal parts patience
and worry, watching October lilt to its rest,

feeling christened, swept insistently through bee-flustered
goldenrod. All night that square
imprisoned by lights blown black.
Something forbidden and lean
is induced in me by your
hands, your hair, the flow of your
back, **dark water surrounding**
our floating hold, by lilies,
the listings of a going
of geese. I was calling your

names. You seemed to be swimming
further and further into
the sequence. I followed far
enough to let your quickened pulse for the first time

fill the spaces of my stammering, fill all its
wings' blurred transparence, the dim,
indeterminate sequence
of my seeing. My inept,
yearning hands harvest blighted
reports on star-scarved twilights.
In **this climate of extremes**
all my weary faces ask
what hand burined birds, etched them
as hesitant crossings-out
of comprehensive darkness,
lustrousness burned into
that resist, our histories.
If I've lost those pictures of you I never had,

if consciousness hid them, what assurance of touch
incandesces this cosmos
of integumentations,
guesses, sequences, theses?
Bewildered ghosts who still thirst,
who still desire the spare life
bleak north sings itself raw for,
these birds, small blue things betrayed,
wrapped in their rivers of silk,
hope, like me, to tell of night,
unmeant thoughts imposed on sleep
that frame **some larger logic**.
This uninhibited room,
a penalty paid for grammar, inclines our thought

to premonitions invisible but present.
These lisped and stuttered listings
emaciate me the way
limping arabesques of dust
unravel things here: stray stars,
bland luck, dirt road headed home,
earth tones and siennas, sleep,
its detail-strewn turbulence
proof that memory cheats truth.
The process calls for bodies
terrible petals snowing
all night into a landscape
that outwaits all the skewed girls.
Sequence healed our war-poisoned earth by alchemy

as if somewhere a fire-fostered sister sequence
meant to insist on strange stars'
varying light. Imagine
all this otherwise, give it
your own sense-distorted twist:
unaccountable yellows,
red delicacies wild as
lovers quarreling over
how it was for the short span
of their mutual dream. Let
trees try resisting the wind,
let storms leave their earth-spiced air
for my disfigurement. All
winter your hands feel lies. Everything threatens snow,

though I still insist intelligence is latticed,
quartz-clastic and quarantined,
unfazed by enormities
measured by matchlight as frail

as falcon-call and as fierce,
untouched by your voice listing
sequences of mysteries:
teal in marsh reeds one sun-shot
morning, drops on a woodstove,
a swift surprise of minnows.
I drowse away each winter.
It happened this way: your name
overcame the only world
I had imagined. The lonely face of God strayed

through the redwoods, disguised as mandalas dusted
on moths' wings. Sunlight sequenced
sandstone hills. I admit
I'm still afraid of faces.
There are **too many pieces**
to my idea, I must
be someone else. All those strings
imply terrible distance.
The trees encase small birds' fears,
ecstasies of rock, numbers'
stutter, the years' logic lost
to inattention. I want
rhythm to match the unveiled:
fenceposts covered with moss, entire tall hollyhocks

overcome with their own color. Not everyone
prays for fire. Some souls linger
with griefs under cold cinders
that suffocate them as skies
suffocate cities, force on
them the rules of rule. When she
fell asleep, my life began
building this house which does not

exist, in the valley of
long shadows. Apparently
I want to sequence myself,
kneel down to drink error from
a ditch gray with grass, with bribes
I **exchanged for blooms** like small spent faces. I tried

to handle hard necessities first, to become
a bird, preferably an owl
because it stays so dark here
where her dreams rain on my dreams,
and all withdraw to the woods,
all the third things together.
Once the flowers withered, I
changed back into my lost self.
I wasn't the only one.
Here are my tears, jeweled blue.
My shadows plan to return
to places no god would know,
where these sequences begin.
That colder, deeper, unilluminated place,

nightshade's nectar and dark, undid my flesh with yours.
The shadowy street, rain blown
down this rubbled wynd, wet soot
staining my love's carved name gray:
all corruptions tungsten-tinged.
Dark, dishonorable scars
inhale brevity from your
dissolving sequences. It
did not last, our happiness.
What passes passes swiftly:
roofs of short-tempered cities,
your sorrowful eyes (**sparrows**

at their dust-baths), my embrace,
your troubled sleep, my world leveled by my yearning,

awash with blushing textures, your hips, lipped lilies,
sex as song. I feel lost here
with just sequence to correct
my view. Against so much glass
starlight shuts a harsh door. On
this my tentative guitar
to tell by touch the passage
to the river is to feel,
obliquely on your body,
the airs I sing. **There is no**
avoiding oblivion,
even for embodied gods,
horses grazing side by side.
The hand that anticipated everything—

shining lamps lined along empty streets, our naked
bodies, brief insect-covered
moons, waiting without hope for
hope, trees lost from one numbered
forest, sheened nashki of waves,
impossible decorum—
heard **weariness in judgment**,
its call-down of cirrus wisps
scrimshawed on beach-bleached femur.
There's no logic to my loves:
your figure, grass in the shade,
sleep, the sea, pelicans' wings,
sequence itself, silver and
frozen. Once the song ends, the sung-of world resumes

its **complications of meaning**, silence awash
with tunnel-damp graffiti,

junctured by saturation.
These fragments are ghost pieces,
ashes drifted down denser
than mountain fog or sea spray.
They are made by strict method,
old newspapers blown across
a field, seepage and stipple,
landscapes pocked pink with foxgloves.
Conspicuous sequences
bear inverse enormities
of fractions numbered past sense,
and dust this glassed-in space I keep trying to name

for the clear air overhead, its pearl-perfect
impossibility too
beautiful to leave alone.
I tell complicated lies,
illuminations brought back
from the fields as quail feathers
gathered to make you new wings,
to map out **all the switchbacks**
between your body and God.
Until sequences fit, we
trace and retrace our dirt lines.
Your body, so nearly free,
pulls me backward from the shore,
salts the air with gulls' calls. Once I thought in terms of

dwarf pines and yellowing valley and quiet pond,
I tried to replace my life
with red-bent light, wind rising,
earth surrendering moisture
to parched sky without concern.
What good does sequence do us

beyond spilling chilled brothers
from this tiny house, these rooms
gracelessly sliding away?
When she mistakes rain for love,
he hides his desire to fly
from the euclidean fear
beyond **the opposite hills**.
Suppose their story just ends, suddenly insists

it's enough, this strewn straw holding mud to the path,
wind jeweled juniper-blue.
Let me re-state the question.
What bends light, if cliffs of sleet
bend willows down to water?
One brittle stick above snow
holds sequence in place. **This shrine
built from** sleep's misplaced relics,
beckons angels to rustle
your other body to song.
I take liberties with names,
almanacs and star charts, lace
(cousin to the dragonflies),
and still you list with reticence, imitating

not **the storm itself** but its offices. I hear
your singing, something to do
with sunlight, with the first signs
of thaw, the sky from inside,
a calling-out bent once then
bent again, burned-out beach homes
outlining sand, the first snow
been and gone, water brought up
from the spring, a boat adrift,
last lilies bent, breeze-blistered

to their inevitable
dismantling. I lose track,
being lonely, old, and mad.
l am that stretch of spurred sequence inside closed doors

that block the night from the night. In love with sagebrush
and sandalwood, your body's
gift of spice-scented prayers,
I sing hymns informed by mango
and lotus blossom, your glow
of almonds, plums, salty air.
I am descanting on you,
musical, invented one.
I avalanche at your touch,
frenzied descent to sequence,
the forbidden dissonance.
In all my imaginings
I imagine your body,
rosy pearl and word. Lost in brilliant blinding need,

I hold the smell of intuition, its call to
spiritual erasure.
What I know counts for nothing:
grease, crushed clover underfoot,
saffron and complicity.
If there was a dream, it's gone.
I see, looking **in your eyes**,
some primitive source of grace
traced already in the words
I was saying as I was
saying them, gone that moment
of irresistible dusk,
coal dust tracked across coal dust.
l keep trying to sequence this loss, but it seems

an algebraic question, of no use to me.
We make ourselves cry. There are
no rules for sequence except
your tears, the trees in your voice,
those rain-laden souls lit like
the silk curve of your cheekbones,
hesitation, just enough
long-ago to keep my hope
layered and elusive. Rugs,
hardwood, lamps, your cigarettes.
Look hard. What **is more true than**
the smell of that dusty road
my soul, poor bird, spilled like grain?
One winter twilight, unshielded in this world of

counterfeited starshine: deer twisted by headlights,
brief familiarity
gradually unraveled.
My lust for memory cooled,
but still I wake carrying
those woods in my head. I once
felt you speak to me, felt you
make of my fingers the truth,
reinvent my hands with your
wounded body, meadows grown
yellow-brown, dusted dry with
goldenrod. Outside the world
that you alone believe in,
nothing is not sequence. In this world I am yours,

entirely contained by your gaze. All things that don't
belong to me flourish: rain,
buttercups lamenting bird-
laden maples, high summer,

sequence **clouded with flowers,**
your face, your voice, your fingers.
Are you close enough to hear
this my slanted life arc from
solitude to solitude?
Whatever else you taught, you
taught me to recall all choirs
of small things, infant ghosts in
apple trees, roses crusted
with light. Your belly unburdens me of the world,

unthinks my voiced world to moonlight fled underground.
Think of my body as a
system of substitutions,
a burning of dreams taken
too far, a miserable
progression from snow to sand,
sequencing substituted
for adequate theory,
lace unwoven by lightning,
methodology postponed,
small birds shrilling my decline.
I can't remember now
why the sky is such pale blue.
l refuse to be forgiven, I don't want to

ask for assurance. The planet, intensified
by contagion and chaos,
the cocked dangers of contact,
abandoned bombed-out places.
Strange semaphores argue for
these sequential lustrations,
her **ravished, needy music**.
In her terror for love she

wants other solar systems
and a former century.
Rain, poor orphan, spirals from
skies forgiven by eclipse.
How will bodies give account
of the coughed provocations of architecture,

the wish-ticking of rough sacred ruins, layered
on past layers, beyond grief,
murdered meticulously?
While the victims freed themselves
from birds and their absences,
my body learned that the tips
of your fingers regulate
hurricanes. They know the small
serious difference between
pour and spill, they can sustain
a leaf floating on a pond.
My topic is refraction,
ghost names sequenced. I recall
more about some birds than about my wife's body

in the embrace her suffering no longer longed for.
This loss-laced life has taught me
to reconstruct salvation
of and in the body, with
ice crucial to a weather-
broken barn, the lean gone moon.
I find new dispensation
in your shoulders. Sequences
rising and falling out of
rebuilt dreams disclose your flight.
You promise emerald light.
I write you the math of my

thousand longings, the fertile
kindling impermanence of unfamiliar names,

brush of your hands, a phrase, this world's hollow logic,
our eternity of need.
You say reeds form no system,
I say souls spill as sand spills.
Who cannot follow the flight
of birds spread like breath
cannot mimic, in the sweet
winter morning light, star-fall.
Imagine sequential light
isolated from your names,
those insistences whose bones,
broken, reach heavenward for
some harder truth, a voice
against which to measure this world's every wound,

long-shadowed space, each leaf-kiss, those fragmentary
outlines we call the real world,
music, thought. **Imagine my
life legible** to others,
crystallizing into quartz,
a match scratched down your wingbones.
Is love a mistranslation?
The question you keep asking
resists my poor dust-crusted
calculus, its rules structured
with rushed singularities,
pendant flowers, jade beads,
wrens, the storm wheeling over
my life. To consider the whole of the sequence,

MATERIAL IMPLICATION

If on safari one may see
a bare-faced go-away bird
or lilac-breasted roller,
and if weaverbirds, flagrant
as finches, fill flame trees
with nests like felted fruit, then

I reject less refractory logic.
I name you Thetis of the shining breasts,
not because, windshield-warmed mornings, sun-slick,
they out-round round earth's runway-graded easts,
not for some angry, doomed, half-human son,
not for your water-life (snowy egret,
cattails, dragonfly), not for those seven
years we waited, regret kissing regret.
One lost sock. What matters goes its own way.
Someone downstreet sawing, someone's neighbor
limping her dog. Dog-hued sawdust terrain
on Mars. All I failed to fail to tell her.
That planet. My impotence to explain.
Dog-warm water-like light. Non sequitur.

If in a row of tract houses
that grid the descent into Cleveland,
a dump truck parked diagonally
occupies a whole front yard, then

a woman bows, turns her back to the wind,
feeds hatchlings in her nested hands, warms them
with her breath, but it's so hot this far end
of spring she must be lighting a Salem

instead, three blood-crusted purple knuckles,
and yes, she exhales, turns, and walks again,
her gait possessing me—everything does—
with another woman as scarred, as thin.
But all that falls as rain tonight will rise
as heat-haze tomorrow when these winds die.
It must be radical contingencies
we call love, the provisionality
of *everything* we call our lives, *bodies*
those Greeks called gods, naked under that sky.

If sixteenth-century Iznik ware
dug up in Damascus mixes
fine white clay with ground quartz, then

how you slip off your shoes, heel to instep,
left foot first, leaving them to form a T,
matters no more, is no more mine to keep,
than two snow shovels still outside, ready,
as drizzle washes June into July
and trims the highway this one afternoon
with strings of headlights, no more than the way
the robin broods, wings spread out, to keep rain
from the eggs, the way her nest rapunzels
its longer, light-colored strands, how water
turns rust from red to brown on the wheelwells
of the plumber's spavined van, the clatter
that damned raccoon makes at night when he spills
the trash. But I will watch you, no matter.

If the Lena River courses north
farther than the Mississippi south,
draining Yablonovyy mountain snow
into the ice-laced Laptev Sea, then

somewhere her eyes' hue must have a rival.
In the geothermal prehistory
of pressure under what became Brazil,
in the igneous light sharp-sifted by
its facet-concentrated chronicle.
In something luminous deep undersea.
In the kincob that confesses quetzal
careening through light-karsted canopy.
Or widow's-mite-offered-us as insects:
a beetle's back prism-tilled minutely;
dragonfly's hexamitos-thrilled thorax;
crushed on my windshield as I drove away,
desire that kept glowing against the dusk,
star-sistered weeping that had been firefly.

If I overhear, interrupted
by breeze-roused leaves and windchimes,
a woman across the street say
into her cellphone **Why the hell**
she ain't say hi back, then *and* **His face**
covered with lipstick and all that shit
and **She be talkin bout she look good**
in skirts and I say Uh-uh, *then*

list your desires, I'll assert your sorrows,
glossed by geese in whose V grief is given,
the marred, moored one-note chorale they compose,
those lost children named again and again,

by the unbreakable fractal code
ferns send not to us or to each other
but to what means mushroom, what suggests shade
and spring, the abstract will that maths feathers,
that occasions the blue-shade-layered hills,
the dread red-shouldered hawk's shagged, haggard head,
missing moss-loosened tiles in the tunnels,
wind-washed sand-white bark-bare branches long dead,
the goose-shade of clouds any breath-blue calls,
the luminous fate coding me, dust-red.

If sunlight reflecting off
the chrome trim of the '48 Ford
in the driveway next door and passing
at a severe angle through the panes
of hundred-year-old glass in my
rented second-story room
makes shivers of light on the wall
that twist the way locust limbs twist, then

thus should the garden have flourished: roses'
reticence the least of it, melting snow
spreading pollen fallen from auroras
south across anthered plains in mud's flood-flow,
bland sandhill cranes accosting Nebraska,
one for one with their doubles, flamingoes
on Nakuru, puffins in Alaska,
each spring peonies the sun séances.
Might have, had I not failed to make it so,
had I felt fewer undiscovered moons
tugging at the tides, fewer fish below
color confined to cool, lime-constant rooms,
had I not heard, seventeen years ago,
cicadas assault each other's one sense.

If silhouetted by sunset
an Amish horse and wagon cross
a bridge over the interstate,
heading north at their own pace, then

I name you Miranda for the wonder
of striped wings, nighthawks that until today
I had not seen hunting since the first year
of my last life, my lost life, now a stray
learning to scavenge after begging failed.
Nothing but totems left me now to mark.
Those birds, that dog, and you—Miranda—lisled
and legible, husk of hunger and work.
I assert you antidote, miracle
of pawprints, proof raccoons pray to the lake,
of four wild turkeys ruthing cornstubble,
of acorns making their peculiar plunk
into water, wonder of sliced apple
fed me, of dreamed storms, grass wet when I wake.

If even under the pine whose roots
choked out all other flowers,
the bleeding heart came back, then

when light cuts across the composition
as at this season, hour, and latitude
it must, nothing is lost on it: linen
scarf framing a face tilted to one side,
candle-grayed plaster, gold brocade curtain,
shallow coin-sized bronze pans poised on a hand-
held balance, tabletop, pearls pouring down
the side of a box, half-sleeves, ermine-trimmed.
Which is to say there is nothing that light
does not love. Certainly nothing of her:

how her half-closed eyelids reiterate
her belly's crescent and her forehead's curve,
how her hand on the table seems to float.
That neck. That chin. Both forearms. Each finger.

If a Babylonian astronomical diary
in cuneiform on a clay tablet
records the observation of Halley's Comet
in September of 164 BCE, then

why not say *cluster of leaves still clinging*
to the tip of one branch (the others bare
that bloomed crimson last week) slowly turning
red to brown, rather than name the lover
who is not here? Why not *bored boy sitting*
on his front steps, sun going down over
the duplex across the street, white siding
letting direct sun send it shades whiter?
Why not savor this porch, call this warm day
girl measuring her front yard, heel to toe,
obsolete antenna on a chimney,
dry leaves in drifts beneath a parked Volvo,
trees trimmed at the top. Why not love the way
even her absence shines, and rustles so?

If the maple in the neighbor's yard
needs trimming, its branches having grown
against the slant of his roof, then

birds first of all: copper-feathered pheasant
collared white, with one curled plume for a crest;
a black-trimmed stork's arced wings and awkward flight;
one sparrow with gold cheeks and a striped breast.
My task today in place of purpose: list

what the world offers me when it withholds
you. Bushes bare of leaves but still aburst
with red berries. Green fields freckled by moles.
One woman standing on a stool, washing
windows; one with a poodle the exact
color of her own hair; two men watching
out a window; one woman shaking out
a rug; a small boy, crying, not waving
at the train so much as reaching for it.

If after her sixth pair of tusks
an elephant dies of starvation,
and if the ants that protect
the whistling acacia
also eat holes in its leaves, then

I will watch for you at the front window
whether or not you are due to arrive.
I once thought I could promise, even know.
I affirmed only what I could believe,
so I believed as much as I could. Now
I want what can't be true, what I must live
under, in a wide field the one shadow,
defying lightning, living a reprieve.
I name you *Ulmus suberosa*
for the improbability of your
standing there, for the fact that you will stay
if and as long as some will another
might call miracle or fate makes it so,
gives you to feed my guardian hunger.

If the tattooed woman ahead of me
in the checkout line, helping her husband
transfer groceries from the cart, wore a long
red ribbon laced through a dozen gold rings
pierced in rows down her exposed back, then

I name you Playing Otter for the way
you walk through snow as if you had never,
as if—so it is—nothing lasts the day,
not least your sleek-skinned self, made for water,
made for swimming, sliding on your belly
down snow-slick embankments and out over
what was beaver pond but not ice yesterday
and may return to scrub by next winter.
We learn from snow ways to know exposed rock,
slanted strata shown by what brief white clings,
transient glazed texture wept from each crack,
crystalline score for what Aurora sings,
the glittering, against our normal lack,
of lovely, otherwise faraway things.

BIRDS

"Birds are thoughts," Willie said.

"Oh," Liberty exclaimed, hurt. "Don't be so indifferent. 'Birds are thoughts.' They're not thoughts."

"Why, sure they are," Willie said. "You didn't think that birds were all they were."

Though What Falls Fall Hard to Hard Ground, Yet May Birds Nest Among Flowers, Flowers Grow in the Sky

The desperate man entered the patio backward,
watching with wide eyes the arched doorway he had just backed through.
Three or four steps in, he stopped, adopting a tense stance,
almost a crouch, not yet having given even a glance
inside the space he'd entered, so intent was he
on steadying with his right hand the pistol in his left,
at eye level and at arm's length, pointed back through the door.
The quiet man was seated near enough to hear
the nervous man breathe, rapid shallow gasps like those
the quiet man's ex-wife had choked out late at night
those last months together, thinking to keep her weeping secret,
thinking his not turning to her meant he was sleeping.

Slate-gray songbirds the size of sparrows had been bustling about,
gathering twigs and twine the quiet man in each case
had not seen until a bird picked it up, small necessities
of their lives the birds brought into being where before
had been nothing. Periodically one would dip to the bricks
and return with a prize to the bougainvillea overhead.

Back home the quiet man would have called this place a courtyard,
but here they called it *el patio*. That every building
had one meant, he thought, this town was made mostly of empty space.
To him, *patio* meant a concrete slab barely big enough
for a glider and a barbecue grill, by the back door
of a fifties two-bedroom that some factory worker
like his father had bought in the sixties, never guessing
he'd be out of work before he had a heart attack,
and have that heart attack before he paid off the mortgage.
Here, though, the bricks that paved the patio still lay flat,
had not been torqued over time by tree roots, those urgencies
that conspired with ice to crack and buckle the concrete.

He had been watching the birds will twigs into existence
for twenty minutes at least when the woman had limped in
and sat at the table nearest the entrance. That short distance
had not been enough to confirm his impression
that one of her legs must be shorter than the other.
Maybe she just had a sore ankle. She seemed surely
his age at least, yet her body seemed bored by gravity
and barely obedient to it, ready any moment
to rise, unlike his body's inexorable sinking,
turning inert, morphing, he thought, into a tortoise.

Except for his job—really, *including* his job—
he did little else now but sit, as he had been doing
this day at one of the nine small tables in the patio:
rough, unfinished affairs, their surfaces badly warped,
as if each 1x6 wanted to become a boat
and be borne away by the waves. Water stains bleached
all the legs at the base. The table nearest the door,
at which the woman had sat, was one of two with only
three chairs. He thought the woman must be, like him, a foreigner,
because the locals, to whom this library's newspapers
mattered more than its books, all read in the rooms with stacks.
Her necklace was much too big, and fake: oval-shaped
plastic beads of simulated amber, one big bead
with a dozen smaller strung on either side.

Once in a while a light breeze would loose a magenta blossom
to drift down from the bougainvillea, whose trunks
gnarled their way up the west wall to overhead wires,
which supported the branches but sagged under their weight.
Sunlight through the leaves warmed the east wall with a thousand ovals
of brilliant white. Between breezes what drifted down
from the flowers was chanting from a distant demonstration,
a phrase from a bullhorn repeated by a crowd.

The quiet man had known, moments before the armed man entered,
that something was wrong. All afternoon a blind singer,
seated on the sidewalk in shade near the library's entrance,
leaning back against its outside wall, had been strumming
a guitar to supplement his grizzled voice. Once,
he had paused between songs, and shuffled through the patio
to the restroom, guided by the library's guard.
He had made his way back outside without a guide,
step by deliberate step, using his cane,
not the slender white kind designed for the blind
to hold before them and tap lightly side to side,
but a heavy walking cane stained dark, struck hard against the bricks,
straight down as if testing whether they would hold his weight,
slight though he was, and then trusted against his teetering.
After a time, the singing began again,
accompanied by infrequent clinks into his busker's can
of five-peso coins. A few seconds before the armed man
had entered the patio, though, the singer
had stopped abruptly, in the middle of a song.

The woman had ignored the armed man's entry into the room,
as she had ignored everything else except her own work,
taking notes from a book she propped open at the top
with the weight of another book and at the bottom
with her spread fingers, intermittently chewing
the blue cap of her ballpoint. The strange silence, though,
inhabited only by the man's gasping, led her
after a few seconds to look up, just before the people
in reading rooms with windows or doors onto the patio
began scrambling for cover. When she raised her head,
the armed man turned his. He looked back for one more second
toward the farther door where his pistol was aimed,
then turned, grabbed the woman by her neck with his right arm,
and held the gun to her left temple. When he pulled her upright,

her chair fell backward and her necklace broke, scattering beads
across the bricks. As the man was forcing her between himself
and the door, her chin, in the crook of his elbow,
was lifted up and her head thrown back, but once she was standing
the man loosened his grip to let her chin rest on his elbow.

He secured her as his shield just before shouting began
from the outer entrance. His holding the gun
against her temple steadied it, but as if he were mute
he made no reply to the shouting. A thin line of blood
trailed down her chin from where she had bitten her lip
when her head was snapped back. Though she couldn't move her head,
she turned her eyes from the doorway as far as she could
into the patio, to find the quiet man's eyes,
which, though they knew blood would pool on the patio bricks,
knew something valiant needed doing, something human,
did not even meet her pleading gaze with feigned assurance,
offered no more solace or aid than the birds, which stayed silent
in the flowers overhead until the first shot was fired.

THIS PARTICULAR EDEN

Drizzle sounds on the garbage bag
taped around the window air conditioner
like leaves on long bamboo shoots
slung over a boy's shoulder
teasing each other as he walks.
Rain measures hope against memory.
The man's fingers float the runnel
down his sleeping lover's back.

The sound of drizzle lazy on the bag
that sags around the window air conditioner
reminds the man of his mother
rinsing beans in her dented colander.
Do not let your left hand know
what your right hand is doing.
His fingers ride the rapids
along his sleeping lover's spine.

Rinsing beans beneath the faucet,
his mother rocked them in the same pattern
perforated on the colander.
Rain leans one memory against another.
The twin dimples on his lover's lower back
draw him like eddies, like an undertow.
He numbers to himself forces not to resist:
floodwaters, gravity, ignorance, beauty . . .

Soaked in rain, hope falls back on memory.
The dimples on her sloping lower back
pull like eddies, like a waterfall.
Could he tattoo, he would make her back a garden,
lush and wild, with flowers and many birds:

egrets, herons, hummingbirds, finches, orioles . . .
Where the river divided, it became four rivers,
and the fourth river is the Euphrates.

The third river, whose name is Hiddekel,
courses east past Assyria.
After clouds quit raining, trees persist.
At his touch her back became a garden:
fish in clear water spawning over smooth stones,
riverbanks overflowing with flowers, trees teeming with birds:
kingfishers, buntings, woodpeckers, tanagers, waxwings . . .
Were love less dangerous, by just so much

would danger be less beautiful.
He admires the intricate draftsmanship
and delicate colors of his invention:
fish, flowers, stones, birds, trees, a spiderweb . . .
The name of the second river is Gihon;
it flows around the whole land of Cush.
Each gust insists the leaves drop mist
like a draining colander shaken.

After the drizzle dissipated,
only the cadence of drops down the gutter
numbered the finally visible stars.
If only beauty did not cost a life.
The name of the first is Pishon;
it flows around Havilah, where there is gold.
The gold of that land is good;
bdellium and onyx stone are there.

Drowsiness increased his draftsmanship:
the spiral of the spiderweb drew him
slowly to its motionless center.
Wakefulness is next to godliness.

Love always holds hands with sleep.
Some things are worth a life.
Like light rain, like a woman's back.
The man and woman were naked, and were not ashamed.

Child of Their Old Age

She was inside napping,
her way of dealing with the heat this time of day.
He was rocking
slowly on the porch swing, his way.

They called it the cabin,
their place in old-growth in a clearing near a pond,
small, half-fallen,
but with a view, the hills beyond.

No neighbor visible.
No phone, the nearest store a twenty-minute drive,
visitors all
wild: deer, a fox, in pairs the doves.

When he saw three young men,
sweat-stained, walking up the dirt road toward the place,
he hollered in:
Sarah, honey, you 'wake? Get dressed.

Some men are coming, who
knows why they'd be out here. Have we got tea made up?
Nothing to do
but offer them something and hope

they don't plan on trouble.
I'll walk out to meet them and try to slow them down.
Anything cool
might help them decide to move on.

One of the men lit up
a cigarette. *Mind if I smoke?* he asked, after.
He wore a cap,
stained like the armpits of his shirt.

We got a truck broke down
a mile up the road. Mind if we make a phone call?
        They won't but one
    of us need to come in, is all.

        But all three men came in,
    saying no, they wouldn't mind something cool to drink,
            then yes'm, one
        slice of lime pie *would* give 'em strength.

        Threatened no harm, did none,
    but accepted the ride to town the man offered
            (having no phone).
        But here's where the story gets weird.

        Two or three days later,
    that same truck—they had it running, but it still looked
            the worse for wear—
        came driving up, the three men packed

        in the cab, a fourth man
    seated in the bed. He stayed there. The three got out.
            Met him in town.
        (The same man who'd spoken last visit

        spoke now.) *He was asking*
    after you. We figured if we brought him, we'd know
            if everything
        checked out. If it's ok, we'll go.

        As soon as the fourth man
    left the truck and faced them, they knew. They'd had a son,
            but he had gone
        missing when he was just thirteen.

He'd left no note. Was he
kidnapped? murdered? Had he run away? They never
found a body,
no clues. Police couldn't offer

any hope. Finally,
after five years, they'd had a funeral for him.
Been thirty
years, to the day, since he left home.

Not until tears began
and the parents embraced the son they thought was dead
did the three men
turn their pickup back to the road.

LISTINGS

A journey should start at night and in secret. If those to be left behind must know about and attend the departure their assembly should stay silent. • A life steals from the rich and gives to the poor. A work adds to the available wealth. • Virtuous texts promise blessedness to "he that readeth, and they that hear the words of this prophecy, and keep those things which are written therein." A vicious text would offer no such assurances, not even the Mephistophelean promise of damnation (which, after all, is only the bliss of the guilty). • Not self-disclosure, but self-enclosure: to conceal oneself in beautiful or exemplary ways. • Most writers write only books they have read, and most readers read only books they would write. Wisdom reads what it would not write, genius writes what it has not read. • Like astrologers reading stars, most readers insist books tell us something we don't already know. • No longer content to ignore the voice crying in the wilderness, now we try systematically to eliminate the possibility of its being heard. • Ideas arrive like meteors, not like doves. The force of the impact lasts, not the idea itself, and not the reasoning that follows after. • Like a gas, like language, God expands to fill the space provided. • That its history be consistent with its theology, Christianity, like its founder, had to die.

One lament masks another. • Suicides send warning signals of their despair. As do the good, the healthy, the well-adjusted. • Suicide: revolution against the tyranny of despair. Happiness: tyranny so complete that the reigning despair is not threatened even by revolt. • One who could not even conceive of ending his life may try hard to ruin it. • That retreat alone makes it possible reveals thought as a form of self-preservation. • A prophet cannot bear good news. • Success: not the duration of one's survival but the alterity of one's death. Not to perpetuate the species but to die as an individual. • The dead don't get more dead, but they do get better at it. • Only as the story of a death can the story of a life interest us.

If others understand what you are doing while you are doing it, you're wasting your time. • One must leave all, and only, the messages one cannot leave. • Prophet: in spite of all the evidence. • That which would articulate the abyss must be itself an abyss. • Wisdom, yes, but one must have wisdom already in order to acquire it. • Against argumentation: not whether an idea is accepted, but how and by whom it is entertained, matters. • One invents the ideas one needs; one discovers the ideas one cannot avoid, the ideas one can neither believe nor forget. • Not silence per se, but the conditions under which it alone is appropriate. • To understand would be to isolate the point at which silence becomes necessary. • Equal distribution of leisure destroys: leisure should be reserved exclusively for those who will refuse it.

Were no windows open on eternity, the difference in pressure would shatter the closed ones. • Independence may be unattainable, but not autonomy. One can choose on whom and for what to depend. • Better to make angels (we have too few) than gods (we have too many). • The mind capitulates not to the world but to itself. The world cannot overcome the mind; but then, it need not. • To persist in something futile, that damnable form of attempting the impossible, avoids the risk of failure by making failure certain.

Fire for the cold, words for the impotent. • Only passions, not ideas, produce effects at a distance. • Thought matters as passion, passion as discipline, discipline as courage, courage as beauty, beauty as sorrow, sorrow as thought. • Art changes the geometry of the world, draws us to the edge where the unimagined falls into the unimaginable. • The thinker's task: to make sense of a world. The artist's task: to make of sense a world. • That two people cannot simultaneously center the universe dooms the artist to solitude. • Could we encounter ourselves, we would do so in art. Could we encounter art, we would do so in ourselves. • The artist counts stars through holes in the ceiling while falling through a hole in the floor. • The necessity that drives one person to create has a quantitative measure: how many others it impels to recreate the same thing, for how long afterward. Not popularity, which like a yawn prompts many imitations among its contemporaries, but imposition, which like parental violence commands replication in children and grandchildren. • Genius finds what no one but itself could will, and wills it in defiance of what everyone but itself wills. • Philosophy requires pride, the belief that one is strong enough to win others. Art requires vanity, the belief that one is beautiful enough. • One reasons to stifle resistance. One makes art to defy it. • That extinct totem animal, truth: reason specifies where it would be found if it still

existed, and art describes what the animal would look like if you could get there.
• The writer aims at oracle: voice so profound that its words can never be fully fathomed, so forceful that the world conforms to its will. Every sentence a riddle, every word a fate.

One may deserve an idea, or not deserve it. • If you don't have to be mystified, you can't be. • Unnecessary words pollute. • Our hatred of ideas that oppose those we believe in, and of persons who believe such ideas, results not from our conviction that the opposing idea is wrong, but from our envy of the person for possessing a capacity we do not possess. • The more one knows, the more one can feel. But the more one knows, the less one needs to. The mind most capable of profound feelings is the mind most inclined to refuse them. • People think the indictments they make come from God, as cats think all that moves is alive. • Who will not heed Cassandra's words fears her presence most. • In the face of death, lies lose their interest. The honest are all dead or soon to be killed. Prophets are not the first to whom the future appears, but the first whom death visits. • In a world of explosions, an implosion would multiply its own force by the force of all that surrounds it.

Some want to spread their lives over more space, to see all there is to see; others, to spread their lives over more time, to do all there is to do. • All humans are intolerant of the Other. "Tolerant" individuals recognize affinities between themselves and what is outside them, so the category of the Other for them stays small. • The preference for strangers: one need feel no guilt, one is not killing *them*. • Even about suffering we are intolerant: you must suffer *my* way. I permit only torments I can understand, only what would torment a person like myself. • The most distant stars can be seen only when one's nearest neighbors cannot. • Utopian visions depend on the imagined possibility of change beyond exchange, change untempered by loss. • Enforced inequality inflicts immeasurable damage, but so does enforced equality. • The defeated long for victory; the victorious long for peace; the peaceful long for another war. • War, because privilege brings boredom, and power impunity. The only relief from boredom is to witness a death, so power seeks to impose increasingly spectacular deaths.

Not honesty, exactly, but what one person cannot say to the other. Intimacy finds weight in the gravity of what is proscribed. • Marriage demands of one's imagination enough strength to accommodate the imagination of one other, but no more. • Lovers and friends spend imprisoned lifetimes trying vainly to recover the knowledge they shared in the first glance, the first word. An epistemological error feeds many of our failures, including the institution of marriage: the conception of knowledge by analogy with familiarity instead of immediacy. • Love is catholic. Attachment to a single object indicates not love but the desire to be loved. • The imperative to love one another having proven impossible, let us now pursue the more modest aim of surviving one another. • Marriage damages by suppressing imagination, forbidding the question "what if?" • Love, the decision to find, and the process of finding, everything unlovable in another person. • In a world of hope, every actual event would occasion despair. In a world of love, every action a death. • Love, the condition of willingness to believe any lie about oneself so long the one person to whom one cannot but lie speaks it. • Always an odd number of people on earth. • In contrast to the self-consumption of love, hatred feeds on others, and so grows stronger with its every exercise. • All's fair in love and war not because there are no rules but because the rules cannot be broken. • Preparation for descent into hell would include selection of a wise companion, or a beautiful one.

A mind full of birds helps only one who can fly. • Virtue is a gift of the gods. Unfortunately, there are no gods. • The uncompromising will eventually be compromised. • Ambition and conscience are too close kin for their union to yield any but malformed children. • One is not false for projecting a persona, nor for projecting different personae in different circumstances or to different people, only for allowing others to dictate the choice of persona. It is no lie to act one way for one person and another for another—unless you *have* to be that way for that person. • Conscience, or food. • Original sin: we have a moral obligation to know everything. We, the irremediably ignorant. • When wisdom became impossible, we sought virtue. When virtue became impossible, we sought peace. When peace became impossible, we sought health. Now that health has become impossible, there is nothing left to seek but hope, which has been impossible all along. • Not to love life but to respect it, to be grateful to it, to do it honor. •

Time engenders hope *and* despair: hope because any one time will always be replaced by another, despair because no given time differs from any other. Similarly, time engenders guilt and forgiveness: guilt because no moment ever really leaves, forgiveness because none ever returns.

Hell must be harder to get into than heaven. A benevolent god would accept all who desired entry; a devil would turn away all but the best. The blessed will look down at the damned not with delight and self-satisfaction, but with tormenting curiosity, and not from complete happiness but from inability to look inward, the internal being the site of what could interest only a devil and have use only in hell. • God died not when humans stopped believing, but when they became better than him at killing. • Only the ability to starve ourselves distinguishes us from flies seething above a carcass. • Rationality can be forgiven for leading so reliably to obedience, only because even obedience can be an act of defiance. • Only a pinnacle, from which a step in any direction would be a fall, makes one's shadow longer than oneself in any light. • A capitalist of the soul justifies his greed toward time and thought and energy with the pretense that his soul's acquisitions do not deprive and impoverish the souls of others but accrue to them.

Death of the prophet: when he starts liking the sound of his own voice, and speaking from desire instead of need. • The preface explains why the writer stopped where she did; the postscript apologizes for her not having stopped where she should have. • Neither experience nor knowledge accumulates to wisdom, but regret does. • The hope that calls itself faith, the hope that calls itself action, the hope that calls itself knowledge, the hope that calls itself love, even the hope that calls itself despair, all rival prophecy in uselessness. Neither a prophecy's truth nor a hope's validity verifies itself until after the fact. • Historian and scientist liken past to future, a prophet identifies past with future. • We do not fear for the world in the face of ecological disaster; the roaches and the algae and the tubeworms above hot springs on the ocean floor will live on. We fear for ourselves. We deny about the species what we deny about ourselves: that no one will notice our passing, and even could we be replaced no one would bother to do so. • Not, as the clichés would have it, to live in the present, but to move with facility between past, present, and future, without wearing out one's welcome in any one world. • Our inability to entertain a multiplicity of ideas simultaneously, we call "truth."

That truth confronts one directly does not imply that only truth confronts one directly. That truth confronts one directly does not imply that it confronts one only directly. That truth confronts one directly does not imply that it need not be pursued. • That people believe truth strong shows stupidity stronger. • Not the lover of ideas but the lover of language loves truth. The philosopher's noble lies are not noble; the poet's noble lies are not lies. • Not consistency, but capacity. Not accuracy but inexhaustibility. To be able to assume a persona for whom belief in a given idea would be necessary. • Certain fish return generation after generation to spawn at a place they have not been since birth. Certain bats can detect in perfect darkness the distance, elevation, size, speed, and direction of a moth camouflaged against a backdrop of foliage moving in a breeze. Certain pigeons can return to a specified location after having been transported hundreds of miles blindfold. And we call revelations from our peculiar sensory apparatus "Truth." • Length in the formulation of ideas amounts to an *ad baculum*. • Delphi did not become an oracle because its prophecies were true; its prophecies came true because it was an oracle.

Less Said

Any river gives its edges eddies and wash where water pauses or pools away from the current.

Our acroamatic, heteroclite tradition. Not Plato and Aristotle, Augustine and Descartes, Kant and Hegel, Heidegger and Derrida, the tradition of dialogue and discourse that thinks the longer we talk the more we know, the tradition of Homer and Dante and Wordsworth and Pound that tries to account for the world by accumulation, but the tradition of Heraclitus and Lao Tzu and the Christian mystics and Simone Weil, the tradition of those for whom the less said the better, the scoteinographic tradition that expects words to resonate in darkness but not to illuminate.

Disaster need not offer a moral. The migrating bird burdened by ice in early cold, fallen from its flight path. Sometimes one should *not* learn.

Some silts silhouette heads on pillows, some sediments save the shapes of skeletons in secret for centuries. The fine grain at its patient work, servant to wind and water.

Orphans all.

There to believe in: the ribcage buried beside the bones of the *Tractatus*, its widow, dead nine years later, her testament eight statements instead of seven, but with less muttering in between.

Can anything not poetry say anything about poetry? Can poetry ever have been anything else? A molten flow escapes through the seams where our categories slide against and fold over each other.

Instead of asking how much we must say before we say for certain, as if the longer we sing, the more replete our map, why not ask how much may we omit without not telling the truth, and then stop, without expecting to know, and without claiming to have discovered.

Sooner listen to God tell obscurely of woman than to man tell plainly of God.

Because nothing follows. Corrupt if anything did. *Nothing follows.* A thought we cannot think, since thinking seeks what follows, but which (from what we *can* think) we know must be true. Poetry's incorrigible dishonesty: in poetry one thing *always* follows from another.

The Devil always wins the argument because only the Devil can name God without guilt. Who owes God nothing speaks freely, and the Devil pays his debts.

We speak to gods we believe in, and hear from gods we don't.

So *that* is what poems listen for: *consistent impossibility.* A disturbance in the magnetic field powerful enough to produce light. An unlikely return through the sea to bury your children in the same sand from which you dug yourself out. A migratory cycle no single generation completes. The chatter of playing neighborhood children decayed into song.

Feeding the songbirds. Naming strays. Rising in time to hear the owl. Measuring rainfall. *I mean to say precisely that we have stopped.*

Thinking of one thing you cannot help thinking of everything. Every object includes the universe in its constitution and the laws of its being. Thought consists not in an Aristotelian accumulation but, like perception, which selects the smallest number of sensations from the plethora of possible percepts, a winnowing to the one thing needful. A widow willing to bear the wind to hear the last leaf torn from the tree. An anorexic girl slowly ceding herself to her will to watch the world instead of consuming it.

Look truthfully. Say nothing that can be omitted.
Sing gently. Gently listen.

TOWARD A PRODIGAL LOGIC

Any idea by itself flattens to platitude;
    only the presence of its complement lends it depth.
The eyes' rapid movements fix objects in vision;
    the mind's alternation between ideas settles thought.
Not *my* ideas. Only those I want to formulate, anatomize, honor,
    to overhear as they argue among themselves.
Inability to hold two ideas at once sets the mind's horizon,
    enforces its inevitable failures.
Like words, ideas combine.

Sounds call to other sounds, and our treasures stem from their singing.
    Poetry calls to silence, as relativity to quantum.
Poems pray to gods they can neither name nor know,
    and worry more important things than truth.
We speak through forms,
    as mummies preserved in ice or peat through posture.
Why settle for faith in what form finds,
    when you can insist on the finding?
Demand form, but refuse any offered.

Thought, a fluid, has structure but not form. Always seeking its level,
    it assumes any form offered: rainbarrel, ditch, river, ocean.
Philosophical questions: their form says there must be an answer;
    their content, that there cannot be.
One does not *believe in* a riddle, one tries to solve it.
    Why, then, respond with belief to one's life, the world, or God?
Though disbelief cannot be maintained, and would not bring truth,
    any belief still guarantees falsehood.
Belief suffocates imagination.

Distance and darkness limit, but do not impoverish, vision.
    How subtle are colors in starlight.

Ho skoteinos. Some of us see better in darkness,
    and trust it more.
Words separate us from the world
    more often than they draw us to it.
If something other than words did exist, words could not speak of it.
    We *can* speak of things other than words, but only because they do *not* exist.
The blind, sessile anemone knows the reef well enough.

Temporal order achieves meaning by representing other orders:
    moral, psychological, ontological, sacred.
I can name everything I have given up,
    nothing that I have not.
The philosopher who pursues ideas with ardor learns to distrust the idea of ideas,
    and becomes a poet, one pursued by ideas.
Patience, and attention:
    the idea you wait for may not pass by, but another will.
Of ideas, too, there are hunter/gatherers, farmers, and merchants.

Pursuit of truth pushes the pursuer *farther* from truth,
    unless principled randomness saves the pursuer from her own earnestness.
Any twenty books I could not put down
    for another one I cannot forget.
The worth of an enterprise matches the demand it places on the media of expression:
    the trite can be spoken easily and often.
As elaborately prolonged foreplay gives pleasure,
    so complexly deferred suicide generates art.
Ideas, wary as wolves, must be approached from downwind.

Discoveries occur not from breaking into thought or circulating through it,
    but from leaving it behind.
Thought discloses most
    after it has become something else.
Any given fact matters less in itself than for what it entails for other facts,
    logical possibilities it opens or closes to them.

Thought, wasteful, vain, and idle,
    has no place in the techno-culture of efficiency and profit.
Thought leads to a promised land it may not enter.

The mind functions by substitution (memory for event, word for thing),
    but objects worthy of mensation are sui generis, so no substitute will work.
We cannot avoid self-deception,
    but we can substitute deceptions restlessly and willfully.
Only long, fastidious tending to fruition one's most singular talent
    forgives the indulging of other, unexceptional loves.
In seeking the river's source, twenty minutes' rest undoes an hour's labor,
    as the current draws one back to sea.
The most reasonable reject reason, as the most loving deny love.

That we *arrive* at *conclusions*
    says all we need to know about thought.
Endowment: others' ideas, the principal,
    generate one's own ideas, drawn as interest.
Ideas liberate us, yes,
    but from other ideas that hold us hostage.
One idea calls to another,
    and the idea that *hears* matters.
How little ours are the principles that select and arrange our ideas.

Revelation never costs less than innocence, and often costs more.
    The prophets set the price at happiness; the tragedians, at life itself.
Resistance as revelation:
    the rusting weathervane shows us the wind.
To speak of something beyond oneself tells nothing about the referent,
    but more about oneself than any confession could.
Better that the courage of one's convictions belong to the convictions
    than to the person.
I am the selves I squander, not those I save.

Ideas in the absence of truth,
      truth in place of ideas.
Perhaps *because* they cannot lift our hammers and drills,
      ideas haunt us, unhindered by reality.
Many manifestoes, one at a time,
      made of one's most urgent disbeliefs.
Whether or not it corrupts the truth, prejudice does fail the imagination,
      accepting received fictions instead of creating new ones.
Faith: the delay between falsification and renunciation.

Vital to the oppressed, poetry dies of decoration elsewhere.
      The parrot's colors still flame in the cage, but to what end?
To resemble no other,
      a poem must risk not being a poem.
What do you mean,
      the idea *in* or *behind* a poem?
Melody, mathematical pattern, shape *are* thoughts.
      Bach's *Lute Suites* do not *convey* an idea, they *are* one.
Thought rejects the form that claims it for the form it claims.

History began with us, led to us, will end with us:
      three masks for one mistake.
Civilization: our agreement to be crueler to each other
      than nature is to us.
Humans, the animals whose primary parasites
      belong to their own species.
It's not that the sins of the father find the son,
      but that the son's sins are his search for the father.
The past lost its meaning once the future was over.

New ideas *are* dangerous, not because they corrupt old beliefs,
      but because they *become* old beliefs.
Accuracy and permanence are less useful standards for an idea
      than the inevitability with which it must be left behind.

Dialogue defers violence best when backed by a threat of violence.
    Depth of character matches the tension of one's internal dialogue.
Slug trails glistening in morning sun:
    we see the results of thought, not thought itself.
We recognize ideas as disease only after infection.

How tempting to transform mysteries into truths,
    but the true remains so by being left out of all accounts.
Truth: not itself but love. Love: not itself but truth.
    It must be so: how could what transforms our identity be self-identical?
Which costs more, truth or its lack? How would we know?
    And why would we want to?
Ill will makes me mean.
    A small vocabulary makes me dangerous.
No anticipating a metaphor's effect on either term.

Ideas like sniper fire,
    like melody that makes the buds in the rosette bloom.
Ideas may accompany moral change, amplify it,
    make the subject aware of it, but not cause it.
Ideas matter less than do their distortions.
    An idea—*any* idea—isolates one absolutely.
Nostalgia occurs when affection for some past self
    overcomes the will to create a new one.
We say so much because there are so many things we want not to hear.

Our finitude: we can trade one self for another,
    but not trade back.
Beliefs past hope of harbor,
    abandoned, restless, at sea.
Preparation for thought packs the mind tightly with words.
    Thought itself clears one small space and listens to what words rush in to fill it.
Thought's erratic flight:
    better butterfly than bird.
Self-understanding would be easier if we were self-identical.

To make subjection and rebellion into twins; to attain not the mind's fullness, but its most meticulously prepared emptiness. To hear not words that have been spoken, but those that should have been. To track the most feral and solitary thought. To balance courage to follow my instincts with the wisdom not to, desire for transcendence with love of the mundane. To bear the responsibilities of omniscience though I know nothing.

To know once for all what I cannot do, but never quite to know what I can. To do well what a simple recursive machine could not do better. Never to underestimate the transformative power of defeat. To attend, as one who longs for rain watches the sky and listens for distant thunder. To be drawn by something inarticulate but precise, as homing pigeons and salmon and sea turtles are drawn by magnetism and the seasons and their own bodies.

Not to be content with one falsehood but to gather many. To permit myself only lies that underwrite renewal, that reveal lies as lies. To renounce, now and often, all that I have said before, and to say what must be said *and* what must be unsaid. Not to fall into nihilism but to dive. To defy sense, in fulfillment of a commitment to clarity. To find a place I recognize but cannot name, *another* world identical to our own, a place so strange that there my life must begin again.

To account for each hour *because* life cannot but be wasted. To fish some life daily from the void. To extend indefinitely the lag between lightning and thunder. To hear the work that calls for my life, though it not have the loudest voice. To follow God into the desert, form deep into the caves, though no one find my papyrus or my paintings for five thousand years.

To attain modesty by sacrificing humility with vanity. To master desires not by subduing them but by elevating them. To live a melody line, or better a chord progression or counterpoint. Not to let love's blurred edges prevent its achieving direction. To muster patience enough to wait at the base of the tree until the prey falls. To ask philosophical questions, without philosophical method. To have one idea, any idea, often enough to get it right.

To register, to hoard, to let wisdom accumulate if it will. To make a mental life of movement and energy, not to wither into one idea. To occupy a position no one else has occupied, or could. To remain outside the gravitational field of sanction. To resist the temptation to seek approbation and support, and to remember, should it come, to watch it warily.

To build, not purchase or inherit, the house in which my mind will eat and sleep and shit and watch sunsets and make love and wash dishes and rock in front of a fire on cold days. To hold each brick in my own hands, turn it over, look through its holes. To level the floors, plumb the walls, wire the fixtures. To know what the land was like before the house. To make my own hopes and plans decide what trees must be sacrificed to make way for it. To make it my own leaks in its roof, my own cracks in its basement floor, and my own ghost that haunts it after I am gone.

Art and the vices share presumption as their precondition.
        Pharisees and poets: even God ought to treasure my work.
Artistic sins: obsession, self-absorption, grandiose ambition, restlessness.
        Artistic virtues: obsession, self-absorption, grandiose ambition, restlessness.
Ideas matter less when one understands them
        than when one does not.
Ideas like lovers demand the attention of one's whole body,
        and must be seduced.
Attention opens the void from which ideas are drawn.

The labor of construction prevents fewer people from building reflective lives
        than does the demolition that precedes and prepares for it.
Though we never cross the divide, the manner of our trying
        may mean life or death to those looking at us from the other side.
Eyes follow movement and fingers flee heat.
        The attention I wish to heighten starts with *resistance* to attention.
We fail to understand the ideas of others,
        as we fail to grasp the consequences of our own ideas.
An explanation of an idea is a different idea.

As narrative needs plot but settles for spectacle,
        so reason falls for coherences instead of the scissions it needs.

The mind must multiply its contradictions:
    hoard and spend, burrow and survey, hide and seek, obey and overthrow.
Reason calls for its own head:
    only unreason could think itself reasonable for consistently pursuing reason.
Like tags on a dog's collar,
    words' sounds show the sentence's movement.
Two parts information, three parts invention.

Between the aims we long for and the world's aimlessness
    stands a gap hope and happiness deny, that poetry tries to name.
Truth: a liquid we skim across,
    suspended only by surface tension, prey from above or below.
Any attention draws the object out of its surroundings into one's own.
    Perceptual space cannot be separated from *conceptual*.
Love, from the basest possible motives, must be *made* noble.
    In this indifferent universe, love, like justice, must defy truth.
Not whether we discover order, but what *method* of discovery.

Lives, like sentences, have pitch and rhythm, are in tune or out,
    though in lives anacoluthon in one can terminate another.
Not to *follow* principles consistently
    but to choose or invent principles over and over.
Looking across the abyss between principle and application
    one hears loose stones fall down the cliff face but hit no river below.
Between rule and instance we hang,
    metal between magnets.
In relation to others we find the distances within ourselves.

One writes from necessity, without knowing it *as* necessity,
    and so without relief from constantly renewed decision.
Whatever other writers request of readers,
    poets ask for an act of imagination equal to their own.
It is hard *not* to say what you mean,
    though the poet must try.

Philosophy: anorexic ideas that wish to be rid of the body.

   Poetry: bulimic ideas, overrun by the body. Either way, thought is fatal.

Staredown with nihilism. First to blink loses.

One who knows the sound of God's voice can hear only the voice he expects.

   One who does not know God's voice cannot distinguish it from others.

God's silence *is* a commandment.

   God's absence makes my defiance identical to my praise.

The degree of the damage determines which lies one takes for truths.

   The nature of the damage determines which lies one loves as lies.

We come bearing prejudices,

   useless gifts to the infant king.

Defenders of the truth believe in truths that need defense.

No place words cannot lead,

   and no place they *will* not lead.

The purer a poet's privacy

   the longer the poems will take to find fit audience.

There are *only* minor prophets. To be heard more widely,

   one would need to commit the sins against which prophets speak.

Philosophers who leave the body behind

   resent poets for bringing it along on the soul's journey.

Purer than excess balance may be, but less beautiful.

Beauty thrives, like anaerobic bacteria or ocean-floor tubeworms,

   even in the absence of apparent preconditions for life.

Even when it is easy to arrive at the end,

   it may be hard to recognize the end *as* the end.

The number of ideas one has

   matters more than which ones they are.

A mind free enough to flit bud to bud learning new dances like bees,

   but bound to bring back pollen for the hive to translate into honey.

Minds, stars suspended in space by attraction to other stars.

First Term

January 2001

The principle here is a basic one:
children must be tested every year.
My administration has no greater
priority than education.
I will work to build a single nation
of justice and opportunity.
The dogs seem to have adjusted. I worry:
one year, you may test and everything is fine.
I'm going to protect that privilege.
Every child must be taught these principles:
we will build our defenses beyond challenge,
we'll see how that affects possible arms talks.
In four years, you measure again,
and all of a sudden something isn't fine.

Interleaf

No one is *not* engaged in this struggle.
Infidels make religious choice financial,
but the martyrs make their faith physical.

Afraid to make their conflicts physical,
America is not fit for a struggle:
their only unity is financial.

Strike America's heart, the financial,
and its swift collapse will be physical.
It will fall after the merest struggle.

So the struggle is both financial and physical.

July 2001

I'm committing this nation to a more peaceful world.
America . . . needs your help by you all living good.
Tolerance is the defining issue for our world.
    We're going to keep the pressure on Iraq.

Our nation has always been guided by a moral compass.
Conquering poverty creates new customers:
it's a defense, as opposed to relying on peace.
    We're going to keep the pressure on Iraq.

Cultures and hope change as a result of our compassion.
You're free to worship any religion,
But the market ought to make that decision.
    We're going to keep the pressure on Iraq.

The next ten years will bring more forms of crime . . .
from beyond our borders and within them.
We will pursue a world of tolerance and freedom.
    We're going to keep the pressure on Iraq.

We should not fear faith in our society.
There are new threats in the twenty-first century,
some things that are unacceptable to me.
    We're going to keep the pressure on Iraq.

I understand politics pretty well,
the power of truth to overcome evil.
To rid the world of blackmail, terrorist blackmail,
    we're going to keep the pressure on Iraq.

I'm very open-minded on the subject.
We're more than willing to cooperate.
I thought that our military should be used to fight.
    We're going to keep the pressure on Iraq.

I'm a proud man to be the nation,
to kind of continue our general conversation.
When I'm ready, I will lay out my decision:
     we're going to keep the pressure on Iraq.

Interleaf

They have no authority over Muslims,
these apostate rulers who defy God.

Freedom cannot be the highest aim
of a people who would obey God.

Neither can peace be the highest aim
of a people who would obey God.

We do not seek the democracy
you would impose. We are ruled by God.

We are not bound to submit to you.
We submit first and only to God.

We do not fear death. We do not fear war.
We do not fear you. We fear only God.

Bin Laden does not defer to you.
Bin Laden defers only to God.

September 2001

Our country will . . . not be cowed by terrorists,
by people who don't share the same values we share.
Those responsible for these cowardly acts
hate our values; they hate what America stands for.
We can't let terrorism dictate our course of action.
We're a nation that has fabulous values:

as a nation of good folks, we're going to hunt them down,
and we're going to find them, and . . . bring them to justice.
Either you are with us, or you are with the terrorists.
They're flat evil. They have no justification.
There is universal support for what we intend.
Americans are asking: What is expected of us?
I ask you to live your lives, and hug your children.
Go back to work. Get down to Disney World.

Interleaf

Are human beings free only in the U.S.?
Can it alone retaliate against injustice?
As you violate our security, so we violate yours.

Manhattan was not the first atrocity.
Lebanon 1982: third fleet, Israelis.
We have been fighting you because we *are free.*

Deceiving yourself about the real reasons
for one disaster only invites a second.
Does a crocodile understand anything other than weapons?

Again and again he claims to know our reason,
and tells you we attacked because we hate freedom.
Perhaps he can tell us why we did not attack Sweden.

January 2002

I will not wait on events, while dangers gather.
These evil ones still want to hit us.
The enemy still lurks out there.
These are facts, not theories.
We'll get 'em. We're going to get 'em.
Our nation must invest in procurement accounts.

I can't tell you how proud I am
of our commitment to values.
Fight on, America. I love you.
Our first priority is to the military
when it comes to the defense of our great land,
but there are some other things you can do:
find somebody who is shut-in, and say,
I'd like to just love you for a second.

Interleaf

How angry America gets
when it attacks people and those people resist!
All religions allow self-defense.
Not only Muslims, but Christians, Jews, even Buddhists
may defend themselves. The Koreans
defended themselves, as did the Vietnamese.
So to answer your question, yes,
I have incited to *jihad* all my Muslim brothers.
May God accept as martyrs
all who have died or been captured practicing resistance.
Khaled al-Sa'id, Abd al-Aziz,
Maslah al-Shamrani, Riyadh al-Hajiri: theirs
is the honor the rest of us missed,
to die for following God's decrees, killing Crusaders.
Other allegations are false,
but incitement to *jihad*, that I have practiced for years
and will keep practicing, by God's grace.

July 2002

There is no wealth without character.
As we prepare our military
the important thing is to restore
confidence to the economy.

To be a patriotic American
we must love our neighbor.
These people, . . . they're poor, and they're downtrodden.
There is no wealth without character.

Help a neighbor in need. I do.
To be a patriotic American
we take lives when we have to.
We worry about weapons of mass destruction.

We take lives when we have to.
We're going to chase them down one by one,
that's what we're going to do,
is to hunt these cold-blooded killers down.

We're a compassionate nation,
and so we're on the hunt.
We're going to chase them down one by one
so long as I'm the President.

Out of the evil . . . will come great good
because I'm the President.
Terrorism is fueled by boundless hatred.
We will offer a fabulous product.

We value life; the enemy hates life.
That's what we're going to do,
defend civilization itself.
This isn't a—the type of war we're all used to.

We do what we do for peace.
It's just a different type of war.
Let me tell you what I think the bill says:
there is no wealth without character.

We need men and women . . . who know the difference
between ambition and destructive greed.

I think that's an important nuance.
Out of the evil . . . will come great good.

We still feel like we're under attack.
The war goes on. We're making progress.
This economy is coming back.
We do what we do for peace.

And so we're on the hunt:
the largest increase in our defense spending
since Ronald Reagan was the President,
to hold people accountable for killing.

We're a compassionate nation,
and the results are better as a result.
You know what's going to happen?
So long as I'm the President

the world will be safer and more peaceful.
You can imagine what that is like,
trying to hold somebody accountable.
We still feel like we're under attack.

I do firmly believe . . . a regime change,
that's what we're going to do.
Not because we seek revenge:
we owe it to history, we owe it to

our children and our grandchildren
to hold somebody accountable,
to hunt these cold-blooded killers down.
It's a great country, because we're great people.

We're prepared for any enemy.
We're not going to worry about process.
The important thing is . . . the economy.
We do what we do for peace.

Interleaf

The Crusader world has agreed to devour us.
The world conspires to consume the Islamic world.
The nations have rallied together against us.

God's book warns against befriending the infidels:
read the exegesis of ibn Kathir.
The Crusader world has agreed to devour us.

"Do not take the Jews and Christians as friends."
This command from God Almighty could not be more clear.
The nations have rallied together against us.

It is our meeting with God for which jihad prepares.
Life in this world is an illusory pleasure.
The Crusader world has agreed to devour us.

We must realize how few are this world's rewards,
that the next world's are more permanent and better.
The nations have rallied together against us.

Arab leaders are fools to seek Christian allies;
except in God there is no strength or power.
The Crusader world has agreed to devour us.
The nations have rallied together against us.

September 2002

I'm here to talk about the greatness of this country.
Why would you hate America?
We didn't do anything to anybody.
　　We believe in peace.

At Guantánamo, all are being treated humanely,
to the extent appropriate
and consistent with military necessity.
　　We love and long for peace.

I don't trust Iraq, and neither should the free world.
There are al Qaeda killers
lurking in the neighborhood.
        I want there to be peace.

Saddam Hussein's regime
is a grave and gathering danger.
He is a significant problem.
        My desire is to achieve peace.

Some up here don't get it, see.
He basically told the United Nations,
your deal don't mean anything to me.
        I long for peace.

One thing is for certain.
I don't know what more evidence we need.
He holds weapons of mass destruction.
        Our job is to keep the peace.

It's time with us to deal with Saddam Hussein.
We must anticipate.
He's a man who has got weapons of mass destruction.
        I want there to be a peaceful world.

The Iraqi regime
possesses biological and chemical weapons.
You can't distinguish between al Qaeda and Saddam.
        My goal is peace. I long for peace.

Saddam Hussein has side-stepped, crawfished, wheedled.
I don't appreciate it one bit.
He is stiffing the world.
        I'm willing to give peace a chance.

It's a different kind of war.
It's a different kind of hater than we're used to.

He has invaded two countries before.
    We're a peaceful people.

This is a man who continually lies.
This is a man who does not know the truth.
This is a man who is a threat to peace.
    The world will thank the United States.

This great country is responding to
al Qaeda and Saddam Hussein.
I can't distinguish between the two.
    To keep the peace, you've got to . . . use force.

In Iraq, they don't believe in liberty.
They think they can outwit us, but they can't.
Haters don't—can't see.
    We love peace and we love freedom.

I'm talking about Iraq.
They should cherish American values.
I want you to know that behind the rhetoric
    is a deep desire for peace.

Interleaf

We are determined, with God's will,
    to continue our struggle,
to build on what we've done before
    against the merchants of war,
but I make this peace proposal,
    a commitment to cease all
operations against any state
    that will keep a pledge not
to attack Muslims or intervene
    in our affairs—even
America. We can reaffirm
    this peace with each new term

of office for its president,
    upon mutual consent.
It will take effect upon departure
    of the last soldier
from Islamic lands. If you choose war,
    we stand ready for war,
if you choose peace, we will keep the peace.
    Now you must make your choice.
To save your own blood is in your powers:
    simply stop spilling ours.

March 2003

America made a decision:
We will not wait for our enemies to strike
before we act against them. Saddam Hussein
is a threat. We're dealing with Iraq.

He has weapons of mass destruction.
We're not going to wait until he does attack.
We . . . don't need anybody's permission.
Our mission is clear, to disarm Iraq.

We will stay on task, my fellow citizens.
It's an old Texas expression, show your cards.
Iraq will be free. One of the big concerns
early on was the Southern oil fields.

I've thought long and hard about the use
of troops. I think about it all the time.
We will . . . protect Iraq's natural resources
from sabotage by a dying regime.

We are coming to bring you food and medicine
and a better life. Do not destroy oil wells.

Our cause is just. We have no ambition.
We have secured more than six hundred oil wells.

Our mission is very clear: disarmament.
God will bless and receive each of the fallen.
Pray for peace. In terms of the dollar amount,
well, we'll let you know here pretty soon.

Interleaf

Don't let their numbers frighten you,
    for their hearts are empty.

Don't let their weapons frighten you,
    for their faith is empty.

Don't let their threats intimidate you,
    for they have not the will
        to carry them out.

Don't let their lies deceive you;
    their self-deception is your weapon.

Don't let their money persuade you;
    it was printed with your brothers' blood.

Don't let their cynicism infect you;
    money has no true friends,
        but looks out only for itself.

Don't let their blasphemy corrupt you;
    they think even God belongs to them.

Don't let their greed corrupt you;
    God is not impressed by possessions.

Don't let their numbers frighten you,
    for their hearts are empty.

July 2003

Our country made the right decision.
We're realists in this administration.
I believe God has called us into action.

First of all, the war on terror goes on.
The first value is, we're all God's children.
Our country made the right decision.

I am confident that Saddam Hussein
had a weapons of mass destruction
program. God has called us into action.

Nobody likes to have the whistle blown.
I think the intelligence I get is darn
good. Our country made the right decision.

I did the right thing. A free Iraq will mean
a peaceful world. My answer is, bring them on.
I believe God has called us into action.

The al Qaeda terrorists still threaten
our country, but they're on the run.
Our country made the right decision.
I believe God has called us into action.

Interleaf

To attentive observers it may seem
that *we and the White House are on the same team,*

bleeding the American economy
to what will soon enough be bankruptcy,

as the mujahidin in Afghanistan
drained to its death the Soviet Union.

It should be plain to Americans
that, though all countries supported inspection,

none of them urged, and few now sanction,
this *groundless war with unknown repercussions,*

but Bush *put his own private interests
ahead of American public interest,*

paying himself and his administration
with no-bid contracts to Halliburton.

*The war went ahead and many were killed.
The American economy bled.*

Iraqis he has killed by the thousands,
but also American youth. Bush's hands

bear the blood of all these casualties,
who died making business for his companies.

Al Qaeda spent five hundred thousand on
what cost America five hundred billion;

Bush and his cronies continue to siphon
billions into pointless occupation.

What al Qaeda did and what Bush chose:
it is the American people who lose.

October 2003

We now see our enemy clearly.
We'll fight them with everything we got.
We believe in decency.
The terrorists continue to plot.
We don't torture people in America.

I don't care what you read about.
They know no rules, they know no law,
but we're incredibly compassionate.
America's ideology
is based upon compassion
and decency and justice.
Nearly every day
we're launching swift precision
raids against the enemies of peace.

Interleaf

That your methods reveal your cowardice
does not restore our women and children
or lessen our suffering over their loss.
What shall we call deaths by enforced starvation?
Is murder only murder as explosion?
Someone in the darkness has to call it night.
Someone has to ask the obvious question:
If self-defense is terrorism, what is legitimate?

That your people believe your cynical lies
doesn't make them true, nor does repetition;
does not make those bombed at evening prayers
in the mosque at Khost less dead, less civilian.
Group our men, call us al Qaeda, Taliban;
are our children any less innocent
than yours, that their deaths should not cause us to mourn?
If self-defense is terrorism, what is legitimate?

Even confrontation with the evidence
cannot overcome your repression.
You substitute denial for conscience.
Three civilians murdered in Afghanistan

as collateral for each American
in the towers. Videotaped, the incident
of Muhammad al Durrah gunned down.
If self-defense is terrorism, what is legitimate?

Riyadh for Iraq, Kashmir, Lebanon.
Cole for occupying our holiest site.
Manhattan for Burma and Palestine.
If self-defense is terrorism, what is legitimate?

February 2004

Every American is threatened.
    Americans always do what is right.
I'm not going to change my opinion.
Every American is threatened.
Look, we need money here. I understand
    my job as your President.
Every American is threatened.
    Americans always do what is right.

We're good at things. By our actions
    we have shown what kind of nation we are.
America believes in elections.
We're good at things. By our actions
terrorists have learned the meaning of justice.
    I made the tough decision to go to war.
We're good at things. By our actions
    we have shown what kind of nation we are.

And I work for free societies
    because I believe in people.
We need money to meet priorities,
and I work for free societies.
I led. Now we're marching to peace.
    Now the world is more peaceful.

And I work for free societies
    because I believe in people.

My attitude is, there's been tremendous
    death and destruction because killers kill.
We . . . continue to open up markets.
My attitude is, there's been tremendous
liberation. We're doing things more wise.
    They are ruthless, and they are resourceful.
My attitude is, there's been tremendous
    death and destruction because killers kill.

We've got kind of a gap in the pipeline,
    but we dealt with it straightforward.
Democratic reform must come from within.
We've got kind of a gap in the pipeline,
but we acted, here in Washington,
    and that changed us, it really did.
We've got kind of a gap in the pipeline,
    but we dealt with it straightforward.

Interleaf

You demand that Americans taken
as prisoners of war be treated well,
by terms of the Geneva Convention,
but you imprison us without trial,
without recourse, without stated cause.
You torture us at Guantánamo Bay.
You accept our surrender at Qunduz,
only to murder us along the way
to prison in Jangi by the hundreds,
packed despite this heat into a boxcar
to die of suffocation and thirst.

You treat your chickens and cattle better.
You like to impose principles and values,
but follow them yourself only when you choose.

August 2004

Lesson one is, there's an enemy
out there. That's why I'm running with Dick Cheney.
We stand for institutions like marriage and family,
which are the foundations of our society,
and that stands in stark contrast to the enemy.
We will lead the world with confidence and moral clarity.
You'll hear me talk about our military
later on and our economy.
In Iraq and Afghanistan we need more money
for our troops, $87 billion more money.
These funds are necessary
to support Operation Iraqi
Freedom. It's our most solemn duty:
ammunition, fuel, spare parts for our military.
This money will buy more armored Humvees.
I think it's a wise use of taxpayers' money,
being on the offense against an enemy.
By serving the ideal of liberty,
we're spreading peace. George Bush and Dick Cheney
are what's best for this country.
Our efforts are unified in priority
and purpose, because there's an enemy
that still wants to harm us. That's the reality
of the world. We spend the people's money
to defeat the terrorist enemy.
It's now providing more energy
for us. The Iraqi people are free.

I will never relent in chasing down the enemy.
These people don't like freedom. You know why?
Because it clashes with their ideology.
And it's really important that we never forget that reality.
We regulate a lot here in Washington, D.C.
We have a solemn responsibility
for the defense of the traditional family.
It's a war in which the enemy is an enemy
that has a dark ideology.
My most solemn duty is to protect our country.
America must take threats seriously.
Deep in my soul, I know that there's an enemy
that lurks and still hates us. We're a free country.
We believe in freedom and liberty.
We got plenty of capability
of dealing with justice. We support free
and fair trade. We're facing an enemy
which has no heart, no compassion. If somebody
has done some wrong in our military,
we'll take care of it. Sound policy
can help unleash the initiative and talent of free
people. We believe in human dignity:
that's the core of our philosophy.
The use of force in Iraq was necessary,
and the $87 billion was necessary
to make our country safer, to make our economy
stronger. Saddam Hussein had the capability
to make weapons. He was a source of great instability,
but for the sake of energy security, Dick Cheney
is solid as a rock. Freedom is the Almighty
God's gift. We must engage the enemy.
We're doing wise things with our military.
We're getting the job done in Washington, D.C.

When you get more products coming into the country,
you can shop. That ought to be the first priority
of any President. That's good trade policy.
Pray for me and Laura and our family.
We're going to do what's necessary
to protect this country. The enemy
attacked us and we got to respond. You see,
when we acted to protect our own security,
we promised to help deliver them from tyranny,
to restore their sovereignty,
and to help set them on the road to liberty.
We've got a fantastic military.
I made the decision to go after the enemy.
May God continue to bless our great country.

Interleaf

Wherever we look, we see the US
as the leader of terrorism and crime.
If a Palestinian, if any Muslim
retaliates, they condemn and attack us.

Gerry Adams can visit the White House;
Ramzi Yousef, they imprison and condemn.
Wherever we look, we see the US
as the leader of terrorism and crime.

Who stations troops at all points of the compass?
Which country has dropped an atomic bomb?
Kabul, Baghdad: who occupies whom?
Who is desperate for whose resources?
Wherever we look, we see the US
as the leader of terrorism and crime.

September 2004

We're getting the job done.
We have overcome a recession.
It was the right decision
to go into Iraq. Saddam Hussein
and the Taliban.
Weapons of mass destruction.

Dick Cheney is a solid citizen.
We have got a plan:
fuel and spare parts and ammunition.
$87 billion.
A struggle of historic proportion.
Weapons of mass destruction.

To everything we know there is a season.
People who want a job can find one.
Our mission in Afghanistan
and Iraq is clear: comfort in
God's promise, which has never been broken.
Weapons of mass destruction.

Interleaf

It is in the interests of Americans
no less than of Arabs to stop those
who shed their own people's blood without remorse
to serve their narrow personal interests.
The war in Iraq is making billions
for those who manufacture weapons
and for other large corporations—
Halliburton and its subsidiaries—

with ties to those who make the decisions.
This is a war begun by the CEOs
of those who receive the no-bid contracts,
the same who help to privatize defense.
Which kills more Americans, our attacks or
the collusion of these merchants of war?

January 2005

America will not impose our own style of government.
Freedom, by its nature, must be chosen.
It is human choices that move events.
America will not impose our own style of government.
Democracy is a prelude to our enemies' defeat.
America's vital interests and our . . . beliefs are now one.
America will not impose our own style of government.
Freedom, by its nature, must be chosen.

FIGURES

I try to channel my pain in a single direction,
to aim it at something moving away from me.
When I make my pain one pain
instead of three or seven it becomes less painful.
When I cannot channel my pain, when they win,
I cannot scream because they will not let me breathe,
and I cannot kill myself because they bind my hands.
They travel together. They circle me, barking.
They hunt at night when only their eyes are visible.
They make the stars. They *are* the stars.
I name them the names they name each other.
They call to each other across me. They speak in code.
They tell each other all my weaknesses. They laugh.
I hear them stalking me. I know which ones
are hunting me before they know I am their prey.
I know their habits, when they feed and how they travel,
but nothing helps except to make them one, so I picture them
single file, eyeing me as they back out of my head
through a distant hole visible as a pinpoint of light.

•

I don't think you understand me.
My grief as a girl over my father's frequent absences
matched my fear of his return.
He taught me not to tell.
My mother taught me not to ask.
I don't think you understand me.
A man's voice carries farther before sundown,
a woman's after. A man's voice carries farther
through air, a woman's through water.
I don't think you understand me.

The few prisoners who survived dismemberment
were forced to eat each other's limbs.
    I don't think you understand.

    •

I have relationship problems. I'm sorry. It's not your fault.
You could have been anyone. It would have ended this way
no matter who you were. Nothing has changed, really.
Nothing about you now is any different than before.
Attraction plays by its own rules. No single feature is yours alone:
plenty of people have your eyes or your voice or your smile.
Why the combination of perfectly common features
that makes you you attracted me how could I know, or why
that combination now repels me. Please do not take this personally.
In some games the rules change while we play. This has happened before.
You knew when we started you were not the first. You had to know.
No one is ever the first. Not even the first is the first.
Whatever happens with the second already happened with the first,
and whatever happened with the first already happened before.
Did you think you would be an exception? It would not matter
what you were like, or what you did, or how you treated me.
You treat me just fine. Only you no longer attract me,
probably because you are not my father. No one is,
anymore. In fact, no one ever was. Certainly not him.
He was always doing things he was not supposed to do,
with people he was not supposed to do them with,
especially me. Then he died, which he was not supposed to do
either, not then anyway, before I could tell him I knew
the whole time he was doing them that he should not have been doing
the things he did with me. Now what am I supposed to do,
and with whom? You see the problem. I am attracted
only when I should not be, to people who should not attract me,
so that now when the consummation of our mutual attraction means

I should continue being attracted to you, that same consummation
means I cannot. My attraction to you could have lasted
only if you had not been attracted to me. I would have spared you
had I known myself in time. I would have warned you
had I myself been warned. I will not trouble you for long.
In fact I will be gone the rest of the time I am here.

•

Do you sometimes lie when it would be easier to tell the truth?
 No, of course not. How could I? Nothing could be easier than lying.
Do you ever catch others in lies they have not yet told?
 Why should what I mean limit what I say?
Do you ever lie to yourself without knowing it? Would you tell me if you did?
 I never let what I mean limit anything I do.
I trust you because you lie to yourself before you lie to me.
 Why live in one world when I can live in many?
Tell me something I already know, and I'll believe you.
 Why be only one person when I can surprise myself?
I trust you because you contradict yourself in interesting ways.
 You trust me not because I tell the truth, but because you do.

•

We regret to inform you that what we have to say
is something you will not want to hear.
We assure you that we did not want to say it,
and that in saying it we mean well.
Please understand that what we have to say
does not reflect on you or on us or on anything
except the regrettable circumstances which dictate
our saying it. We hope it will help to know
that we have had to say the same thing to many others,
though we would rather have said to them then,
as we would rather say to you now, what circumstances
so unfortunately precluded our saying to either.
We hope that soon someone will say to you

what we wish we could say but cannot,
and that in the future that we are sure holds for you
the very thing we ourselves may not provide
you will continue to view us in the same favorable light
as before we were forced to say what we must.

•

    I don't think I love you like I used to.
After he had tightened the knot on his tie
and shrugged his jacket back on,
after he had opened the door,
he said he would not be back.
    I don't think I love you like I used to.
A planet strayed from orbit,
a human child born blind.
A star exploded into color invisible to our eyes.
    I don't think I love you like I used to.
Wind longs for heaven, leaves long for earth:
their love does not last.
    I don't think I love you.

•

I have tired of making sense. I make sense all the time. Everyone says so,
even you, in your own way, though you never come out and say it,
since you never come out and say anything. Not anything you mean.
Mother used to tell me I made sense. That seemed to matter at the time,
the way it matters now whenever you tell me. The kind of mattering that tells me
I have not done what is expected of me, that what is expected of me is impossible,
and that it is my job to discover what is expected because no one will tell me.
Though I am still expected to do it, even if I cannot find out what it is.
Father never told me I made sense, but his was the kind of not telling
that meant not to say everything it did not say, not the kind of not telling
like yours and mother's that means to say what it does not.
Who am I making sense to? No one makes sense to me. Even I,
for all my making sense to others, make precious little sense to myself.

Though, unlike everyone else, I try, very hard. But now
I am through with that, the trying to make sense.
This will make sense later, if it ever makes sense.
It would make more sense if you were me.
A lot of things would make more sense, to me at least,
if you were me, or if at least I were someone else. As in fact I am.
You have always been me more than I have been me.
Unlike me, you always knew what you wanted me to be,
and why I was not what you wanted, and what I could do to change.
Unlike me, you always knew what I meant to say.
You always read in my face glyphs I did not write there
and could not believe when you read them to me.
I know now that making sense only attracts the wrong kind of people.
The kind who want to be things with names, and want to have things
that can be had, the kind who are forever wanting things explained,
the kind who refuse explanations, who because they cannot make sense
envy sense in others, crave it for themselves, track it, spy on it, enforce it.
I do not want to be with anyone I could attract, including you,
whom I once attracted, and still attract in the attenuated sense
in which attraction can be perpetuated. We made sense together,
which is what attraction is, or was with us at least.
When I moved, you moved. But flashes of insight are brief.
If they lasted, so would we. Nothing would change.
Everything would go on just as long as it made sense to continue.

    •

I thought you would tell me if something was wrong.
    I thought you would ask me if you wanted to know.
When there were problems before, you always told me.
    When I told you things before, you never listened.
When things went wrong, you could count on my being there.
    When you were there, I could count on things going wrong.
You should have asked me to leave if I caused such problems.
    You should have left without having to be asked.

I never did anything without first thinking of your happiness.

You never did anything without thinking you were my happiness.

Nothing can take away what we had together.

We had nothing together that you have not already taken away.

•

How did you know what I should feel before I knew I should feel it?
I would believe I should feel what you say I should feel
if you didn't say I should feel it. I would pretend to have the feelings
if I could, to make you happy and so I could believe them myself,
but when I pretend to feel what you say I should feel, it upsets you.
And once you insist I should feel it I can only pretend that I do,
because to really feel what you say I should feel, I would have to feel it
without being told to. I don't know how it became so important to you
that I feel what I didn't know I was not feeling, or how you came to believe
I was feeling what I couldn't possibly feel. What you say I should feel
so closely matches what you say you feel that since I myself can't feel it
I also can't believe you really do. All this time I thought it was enough
that I wanted to make you happy. All this time I thought I could.

•

I don't think I want to anymore.
For years the dog growled, muzzle through the fence
when the woman wheeled her husband past.
The first day she passed by alone,
the dog watched from the porch.

I don't think I want to anymore.
The same salinity that silts our humors
infuses their sister, the sea.
The same lights swim in each.

I don't think I want to anymore.
A drowned man will not sink
until a woman is drowned.

I don't think I want to.

•

She does not have to love him. No one has to.
No one has to love anyone. She couldn't love him if she had to.
Love doesn't work that way. It's not like breathing, for god's sake,
though what you want plays the same role in each.
Love is not like anything: if it were, we would know how it works.
Think what will happen if she doesn't love him. He will go on
being unlovable just like he would have, but he will also be unloved,
and that will be her fault because she could love him.
Her loving him won't keep him from being unlovable,
but it will make the being unlovable his fault,
make him lose sleep at night instead of her.
Except that unlovable people never believe they are,
and besides, her loving him will prove he's not unlovable,
so he will sleep just fine. It will be her losing sleep.
She will be upset that he's not returning her love,
and she will feel guilty about being upset, since she knows
that if she really loved him it wouldn't matter if he returned her love,
so she will be afraid she is not loving him even though she is loving him,
and that will make her fear it's her own fault he is unloved.
It doesn't matter what he's done to her. If she loved him
she wouldn't let that get in the way. That he did what he did to her
proves she is the one who should love him. He could have done it
to anyone. He does it to make up for what he would do
if he were not unlovable. She should learn to like it.

    •

I will be late this evening. Go ahead and have supper without me.
    I will not be here when you get home, whenever that is.
I have a lot of things to finish up here, things that have to get done.
    I will leave a note telling you in general terms where I have gone.
There are things to finish up there, too, I know, but these are easier.
    It will be nowhere you have heard of or would ever want to go.

These things, though they come back later, can at least be made to disappear.
    I will leave directions, but they will lead somewhere else.
Those things never really go away, no matter what I do.
    Somewhere else has always been your favorite place to be.
I feel more comfortable here, where I can sign my name.
    This was your last bad habit. Be proud. I have finally become you.

    •

Don't wait on me, she said. Patience is a virtue,
and you should spend your energy
preserving those few virtues you possess
instead of wasting it chasing new ones.
I can catch up. You go on by yourself,
wherever you are going. You have told me
a thousand times where that is, but I keep forgetting,
and there is no point in telling me
while I am concentrating on getting ready
for whatever we are going to do.
Never mind, though, I will catch up with you,
wherever you are. It won't start without me, whatever it is.
You go on ahead. I have a few things to finish here,
but none important enough to make you wait.
Nothing is important enough to make you wait.
Our going together matters less than your being there.
Your being in such a rush told me that,
and my running late shows I agree.
It is such a long way that you should start now
if you want to be there on time.
Anything could happen along the way.
Something could fall out of the sky.
Something that should work might not.
Something might be in your way.

Leave yourself time for any contingency,
including the possibility that I will decide
not to go wherever you are going, or to be
where you expect me when you return.

·

I don't think I can tonight.
After daring me to lay my hand on the table,
my five-year-old brother broke my finger with a hammer.
I was four. Neither of us knew how badly one person
can hurt another without meaning to.
I don't think I can tonight.
The corpses of everyone who ever starved to death
would reach to the sun and back,
but would not cover the sea floor.
I don't think I can tonight.
The arteries that pass beneath the pelvic bone
into the penis are named Misery and Misery.
I don't think I can.

·

I was never in control. My body left me.
I had to tell it what to do, like having to explain a joke
or tell a lover what you want or interpret a dream,
knowing my instructions were no solution,
only infallible proof that something was wrong.
Everything was happening an instant too late,
like sound arriving always just after the flash.
No one warned me this would happen
or told me how to make it stop.
No one gave me any information I could use.
The rescue parties arrived after I had frozen.
I watched myself do it. I didn't try to stop myself,
since I didn't know what I was doing.

In fact I don't know now what I did,
though I do remember doing it, whatever it was.
I remember what her eyes looked like
the instant I did whatever I did,
and that both of us were scared,
I because I was not in control of myself,
and she because she was not in control of me.
It was not whatever I did that was wrong,
but how and why I did it, and who I did it to.
She knew it was wrong, but couldn't tell me.
She tried to, but I wouldn't listen. I couldn't.
Her words didn't match the movement of her lips.
She was crying, but it didn't sound like crying
or feel like crying until after she stopped.

STAR CHART FOR THE RAINY SEASON

I thirst for God as a doe thirsts for the flowing stream.

The skies sing God's glory, the heavens her handiwork.
Day speaks to day, one night shares knowledge with the next.
With no need of tongue, God's song shades the earth,
wedding baldachin for the sun and his lucent bride.

Daughters of the holy city, spirits of the rain,
guard my love's sleep until her own desire rouses her.

My mourning dove, call your falling notes from the ramage,
for your dark eyes lull me, your voice soothes like cool night rain.
Seal your heart with my heart, knot your legs and arms with mine,
for love is stronger than death, and passion more fierce.
Heavy rain cannot quench love, nor flood wash it away.

                    •   •

I've tried to find a way to tell you what I don't know how to say,
something about a rooftop garden with ornamental trees
organizing the gridded gravel roofs around it, lending to the view
from this room I've never been in some quality I know not to name,
though naming it *hope* would lurch toward the thing I would be thinking
if I knew how to think what I know I want to think,

                                        if I could think
as dogwood petals think, releasing light for their beautiful few days,
calling to birds that haven't lived here since before the tree's seed split,
since before you ushered me out of my last life, which I now know was not a life
but had gardens on the ground, into this life, which is no more a life than the other
though the gardens here grow brighter and smaller and higher,
almost above the birds the dogwoods no longer know how to call,
though call them they must, these birds that know what to say and say it insistently,
the birds I no longer know how to name though they be as vivid,

                                        as gold
and scarlet and indigo, hidden in these trees as they would be held in my hands.

        •

Some nights I awaken caressing myself, running my fingernails lightly
backward across my ribcage, touching the tender parts of one arm
as lightly as I can with the fingertips that end the other arm,
as if I were carrying signals star to star across the constellation you carry.
Sometimes I wake up in ways and at times and for reasons I never did before,
not dreaming so much as thinking, not thinking so much as longing,
writing these love letters—
                              let me call them what they are—
                                                  out of my sleep,
these doves released to cross the waves toward the receding horizon,
not expecting evidence of land, exactly, but to honor its memory.
        •

I've been rising early to meet you here in the park where the rain seldom stops
because the clouds that blow in from the sea can't cross these mountains,
though I know you haunt the part of the park I've been afraid to enter,
fearing I would not find my way out, and anyway I knew you had left
a few lives ago, lives long before mine which after all is hardly a life,
and I knew my reasoning was wrong because what reasoning is not.
I didn't expect to find you or find myself here in this light
that the not-quite-constant rain carries down from wherever the clouds found it
in the shadows of trees older than the places of your even-closer-to-constant pain,
or what would be shadows if these trees taller than my listening for you
were not smothered under hand-urgent clouds now as always,
if this brilliance didn't seem to seep up from the earth itself,
if my logic did not so swiftly, so finally fall apart,
                                      this logic I keep mistaking for love,
as a boy frightened from sleep mistakes shadows thrown by passing cars for wolves,
love I've learned is lonelier than its absence, lonelier than these gasping trees
are graceful in the rain that sounds like your voice I came here wanting to hear
because pain is more beautiful than logic, more beautiful than my image
of these mountains which because clouds always cover them
I know of only when you tell me they are there in that voice I've come here
where I don't live to hear,
                          all this distance from where I normally don't live,
which never had mountains though it always has clouds,

and which does not have your voice that after all I have heard only once
and don't expect to hear ever again, though here I am at the park
not exactly thinking I would find you, having found so little of what I've ever sought
but listening anyway, lost in spite of myself, trying to reason my way out
with logic I know is faulty but which I follow because it sounds like your voice
and because so often I feel like a boy afraid to cry for fear the shadows
will hear and enforce their logic, which would keep me from this park
where though I know you are not here I still listen for your voice.

                    •

Of the several reasons I distrust movies the foremost is that in them
characters do the reckless thing and come to regret what they have done,
but I regret nothing, having done nothing worth regret, nothing reckless ever,
having realized so little of my will, having flown over my desires as a bird migrates
over water whose end it cannot see—
                              emigran y huyen pájaros que dormían en tu alma.
I regret all and only what I have not done, what I failed to do, failed always from some
deeper failing since each of my failings, so many I no longer try to name them
(each deeper than the last),
                              my failings hold one another up as the planets and stars
hold one another in orbit, so here I am failing again, looking down on my desires
that reach to both horizons and call each other by your name.

          •   •

Finding loans more pleasure to labored seeking;
indirection stimulates the seeker's hunger.
God grants truth only to desire.

A STUDY OF THERMODYNAMICS

Lament for the Blood

Strange how little respect you have at bottom
for psychical fact! You nourish the illusion of freedom,
so you cannot explain the most significant
occurrences, like why he chose fire for his threat
who feared three hemophiliac brothers exposed
by transfusion to AIDS, instead of, say, spray paint
or a slaughtered pig scattered across their lawn.
And why after losing custody the mother stabbed one son
exactly thirty-nine times in the chest
instead of twenty-two or forty-seven, then chose
for the other seven times in the chest and nine
in the back. *For me 2, 4, 6, 5 are not just numbers.*
They call up images. They have forms. 1 is firm and complete,
a pointed number, a well-built man;
2 is a haughty woman, rectangular, grayish-white;
3 a rotating segment; 7 a man with sideburns;
8 a stout woman, milky-blue like lime.
But *your* numbers are nothing, they only numb,
like casualty counts on the six o'clock news.
They account neither for themselves nor for their relation
to other details, like why she chose to use
the knife she did. Nothing is without meaning.
To call accidental her choice of a Days Inn
over a Motel 6 dismisses her destruction
and denies the weight of their deaths,
all to preserve the ideas of choice and chance.
Of the many species of pogrom, ignorance
costs most: too many drownings in blood, too many
immolations in unnecessary fire.

Lament for the Lungs

Harsh footfalls in the back yard, late-October-lush
with leaves still brown and brittle, not yet black mush.
Almost fifty years in this house and he has seen
brave the yard, or his wife or grandchildren have seen,
easily two hundred deer but heard none not first
startled to flight by his voice or his fetching firewood.
So it is not hooves now fleeing out of earshot
into the forest across the stirred-up dust
of his interrupted sleep, not leaf-light fox feet,
not a skunk or stray dog that occasions his held
breath and the questions whether to wake his wife
and how to resist that state toward which all things tend:
the man he will find tomorrow, motionless, half
leaf-hidden, hideous and spectral, a surreal end
to some too-vivid dream, one leg bent beneath him, eyes
open, lips blue, frozen on the spot where the frost
from his last breath scarred the starlight like shattered ice.

Lament for the Umbilical Cord

If he finds me, he'll kill me. He has a gun.
But I won't turn him in. I won't turn my own husband in.
So she took the girls and hid. Her promotion,
his unemployment. *I felt it coming. He was proud.*
It was too much for him all at one time.
He went back to the old ways, the old crowd,
he beat her, he started doing drugs again.
He was unscrewing all the vents when we snuck out,
checking the heating ducts for cops he thought were in them,
staked out, after him. So they settled out of court:
he took the past, and left the future to her.
Evil is an absence, a privation.

Evil does not exist; just ask Augustine.
Or, better, get it from the horse's mouth:
Can you reel in Leviathan with a fishhook?
Injustice is its own reward: or so aver
Socrates and the can-man who pedals highway 77 south
of Waco on his battered Schwinn with three green-black
Hefty bags bulging over the basket
like a beer gut over its belt, sweating through a T-shirt
whose faded flock letters read GO TO HELL SATAN.
But the girls know injustice as its children's reward,
how it haunts them like an absent father,
breeds only bastards *who (like forbidden*
wares) creep surreptitiously into the state, so that their
existence as well as their destruction can be ignored.

Lament for the Teeth

I bit him on the nose because what else could I do
with him on top of me punching me in the gut
and me thinking the whole time this wasn't so different
from how sex with her was because back when we did
she liked to sit on top of me and hit me and even though
she was a woman and much smaller than him or even me
she could hit damn hard let me tell you which probably
then made me think of biting since when we were in bed
she liked to bite so when he started screaming I thought
he's doing almost the same thing now he did all last night
while I was in the car hungry and freezing my balls blue
and nothing on the radio because what could interest you
after you've tapped phone calls your wife makes to her lover
and I thought how stupid I must look to the crowd
that gathered pretty quickly from God knows where
and how I need a shave and how my wife who hasn't fucked me
in two years or wanted to in longer than that is kicking me

and I thought no wonder she likes him his prod
must be huge if he's so big I can't get him off of me now
any more than I could keep him off of her last night
and I thought it will cost him less energy now
to send me to the hospital than he spent then getting her hot
while I sat outside in the cold in the car I bought her
to drive to work before she bought her own car
to drive to the apartment this giant who is pounding me
keeps for them to screw in and me wondering all that time
why I was there and what I was going to do when they
came out and what to tell his wife when she calls this p.m.
like she has every day for three weeks to cry over
their kids till I don't feel sorry for either of us anymore.

Lament for the Eyes

Even in dreams the Second Law holds. In his,
a solitary luminous human figure
ascended a steep slope knee-deep in snow,
his feet and legs turning slowly to fire.
It was all he had left to show
for his having been beaten and blinded, for the boys'
having left behind their clubs and his keys and wallet,
for the neighbor's account of their leaving the scene
drunk and laughing, for the first blow feeling exactly
like a door closing on a dark room. As water
is drawn to low ground, substance seeks the state
of greatest disorder. The entropy
of a closed system must always increase:
an unkept aquarium, kids on a bus,
cream poured into a cup of coffee. The lawn will never
mow itself, nor the carport keep itself clean.
And we hurtle helplessly toward chaos,
maximum entropy, the state where absolute disorder

returns to absolute order, where no
change is possible: the heat death of the universe.
So he returned to shavings of radiance
scattered behind him, re-collected them into the glimmer
of small towns seen from the air at night, as weariness
settled on him like chalk dust or feathers or snow.

Lament for the Hands

Someone has to feed the dogs and let them outside
so they don't piss on the floor and put the diaper
on whichever one is in heat and run the sweeper
once a week or so while she's out dancing because
it takes her mind off not dancing which she prefers to avoid
and he's out following her to prove to himself he knows
what she's doing and to make sure he knows who she's
doing it with and someone has to be here at bedtime
to turn on the porch light to keep thieves from taking
any of what the bank will take soon and someone
has to mike the groceries he buys on his way home
from watching whoever's apartment she spent the night in
before he sleeps through the meals the groceries were for
that they can't afford since neither has time for work anymore
and someone has to answer the phone so whoever keeps calling
can hang up like they always do without a word and someone
has to remember this was a mistake a long time
before they knew it was and someone has to tell them
that if they had been as happy then as they insist they were
they could not be as unhappy now as they tell each other
they are not and someone has to remind them I can
watch TV as well with them gone as I can with them home
and someone has to learn to be like somebody besides them
because they won't do it themselves and soon it will be too late.

Lament for the Feet

Except a six-year pony penned from birth
inside a barn, I never seen anything worse.
Eleven Dobermans and mixed breeds, some pups,
removed from a residence after anonymous tips
about a dead dog decomposing on the porch.
Still and yet, this many dogs almost beats that one horse.
The problem of human freedom one might couch
in other terms than Kant's. *It's nasty in there.*
Dog shit everywhere. How could she breathe?
The woman, nearly ninety, wept and pleaded
with the workers. *I've been raising dogs right here*
in this very house since before your mothers were born.
If I'm treating these dogs bad as you say,
why come you need those chokers to drag them away?
The Humane Society truck's radio, left on,
played "Me and Bobby McGee." *They were strays, unwanted.*
I fed them and gave them a home. Now you'll kill them
and call me cruel. And who will protect me?
How will I sleep? The welfare worker
said the woman cannot be forced from her home.
But freedom of will does not free one from necessity
or obligation. The neighbors lost interest soon
and left her lawn. Meanwhile a breeze blows in
from the Gulf on a girl showing friends the spot where
she lost her left foot to a shark. *He kept twisting it*
like a dog with a rag, she says just to hear them squeal.
Really, he only managed to take a chunk and maul
the rest, but the doctors had to amputate.
She had to learn to trust loss. And in Houston
a boy tries to jimmy a padlock with a broom
to free his six-year-old sister from the storage shed
their parents called "the naughty room."

She was causing trouble at school, wetting her bed,
threatening to run away. We made a decision.
We thought a few hours here was best for her.
Police said the girl had been left water.
If not of perpetual peregrination,
at what price purchase the wind and the sun?

Lament for the Genitals

*Fear won't stop them coming to me. You pretend things make sense
if you want to.* Order is not all there is to experience.
Ask the woman who keeps dialing the right number
and reaching the wrong party. *Look, lady, there's no Rose Spence
here. Call the damn operator, would you?
Look it up in the phone book. It's two
in the morning, for Christ's sake.* As if anger
could keep the world from waking him. Or keep
the spirits above the clouds. Instead, they let
their ladders down, they peek under skirts, sleep
between couples, never leave a trace. Even in moonlight,
love casts no shadow. *Love? Love ain't got shit
to do with sex. Love ain't got shit to do with nothing.
Sex is power, man. Sex is food. Sex is pain.*
Sex makes promises love keeps, maybe? Sex is love sleeping
with one eye open? That doesn't ask for explanations?
Or whose extended forecast always calls for rain?
Love suffers no "anatomical extensions,"
has no more intercourse with groups of six
on New Bedford barroom pool tables than it has
with satisfaction or peace. If only love were not
so intractable. If only love listened to reason.
Or could be had as easily as Andreas' peasant woman:
*Lavish praise on her, and when you find a suitable spot
do not scruple to take what you seek and win her embraces*

by force. If only extension and fixation
were as easy for love as for sex.
If only love had to be neither guarded nor guarded against.
If only the lover inherited more than two
empty tumblers, six cigarette butts, the light left on
in the bathroom, one hair on the pillow,
and perhaps a scribbled note stained by the new sun.
Love can be avoided. Love can be lost.
Who leaves at night will never wake alone.

Lament for the Fingers

A study of thermodynamics might include
eighteen illegal aliens trapped in a Texas boxcar.
Officials estimate the temperature
in the airtight compartment reached at least
140 degrees. The sole survivor said the rest
attacked each other like wounded fighting cocks.
I was running from hell but it followed.
Heat, at least, had hunted him. Heat keeps no secrets.
Heat does not lie. Heat speaks from the air, from rocks.
Thus the white flash hotter than the center of the sun
(180 MeV explosive yield
from every fission), thus the hot black rain,
against still-standing cement the silhouettes
of instantly obliterated bodies,
so many secrets suddenly revealed.
Jesus Christ, if people knew what we were doing,
we could have sold tickets for a hundred thousand bucks.
Fire knows all. Fire tells all. Thus the ancient art
of pyromancy; thus the perpetual flares glowing
atop hundreds of Gulf Coast refineries;
Thus the frenzied drums, the sweat, the shimmer of heat
above red-hot coals in the primitive firewalkers' pit.

Or the two boys out past bedtime playing army
near the charred remains of a farm house,
hushed by a sudden tiny incandescence,
a stranger, crouched beside the still-standing chimney,
his phosphor fingers enfolding a flickering, proximate star.
His hoarse voice and hysterical laughter
strangled the words "asylum" and "crematorium."
In the darkness each drag shone, a red firefly
freed from his cigarette. He threatened them
never to tell, and they kept his secret,
even months later when they found him face down
in the creek behind an abandoned mill, heels dry,
his hair hoarfrost, his clothes above the surface set
with ice crystal sequins, winter his ruthless hunter.
Ice conserves whatever it ingests. A cryogen
will not betray a trust. So Jews were stripped, sluiced with water,
left outside unanesthetized all night.
Rascher himself cringed at their cries. *Thank God
it has frozen again at Dachau.* So Kurti, Robinson,
Simon and Spohr cooled a specimen of copper less
than 0.00002 degrees away from perfect stillness,
from a stasis science says cannot be observed,
cannot be reached, but perhaps can be gone beyond.
So the pain of extreme cold pierces like the pain
of burning, and leaves similar scars. So absolute
zero remains a secret, as promised, perfectly preserved.

A Manual of Happiness

Humans fall to grief, surely as birds fly.
Job feared God and turned his face from malice.
He fathered seven sons and three daughters.
Then God spoke to Job from the thunderhead.

1.

Kodiak

I should have owned it as an omen
when I saw my father struck by lightning,
but I was eight, watching from my bedroom
as he walked from his workshop to our house
across the backyard in late afternoon.
I had stopped playing, out of boredom.
No storm stood to, no rain streamed down, no hail.
No lightning followed the bolt that struck him.
Furrowed like the fields my friends' fathers farmed,
with hollows in them like so many ponds,
the mammatus clouds that day mimicked
my world, turned upside down. From that time on
I knew the sky's next note, the way I feel
Bill Evans' chords rise within me and breach.
 My father survived, but part of me died.
Though the lightning bolt itself took no time,
its infernal mental repetitions
swallow me always in slow motion.
Again and again the charge meanders
carelessly from God's clenched fist the way
rivulets rolled down the sloping drive
after my mother opened the spigot

at the side of the house, until she found
the nozzle of the garden hose she stretched
toward the flowers she said her eyes liked
and her nose loved and her hands had to have.
Over and over the bolt repeats itself,
but he never looks up, never sees it.
Always his eyes stay focused straight ahead.
Without explaining why it chose him
instead of the house or his workshop
or one of the nearby trees, the strike
knocks him against his shop, ten feet away.
      Over and over I run downstairs.
Mother leaves Mendelssohn mid-measure
to follow me out. Then I am crying
because the man propped against the tin wall,
the man my mother has just kissed and kissed
more urgently than I had ever seen,
the man whose chest she has just pumped and pumped,
her hands on top of one another
over the fresh burn mark on his T-shirt,
that man does not know her or me. She shivers,
tears like lightning careening down her cheeks.
His swollen soles show red through black, charred socks.
      A map of Alaska smokes, branded on the lawn.

Alaska

My brother Kodiak played piano,
prodigiously. Even in the cold world,
years before my birth, I heard my parents,
standing side by side at the kitchen sink,
fight for their first creation. Father, firm:
He's barely turned seven, for God's sake.
He's in second grade. Let him be a kid.

Mother, mad: *Prodigies can't but be kids.*
It's in the contract. My God, you've heard him:
I work a week on a piece, he plays it
perfectly, first time, by ear. Normal kids
can't do that. Normal adults can't do that.
I've played for twenty years. I had lessons
more years than he's been alive. My mother
sat with me after school for an hour
every day in front of a used upright
that wouldn't hold tune or sound the A#
above middle C. You can't understand.
My child can escape mediocrity.
He has a gift. He can be somebody.
Don't stop him. She washed faster than he rinsed.

      His vision of heaven differed; so did
the soterial role he assigned his son.
What's the problem with mediocrity?
Mediocre runs in my blood. I come
from a long line of mediocre folks
who never attracted much attention,
just worked hard and held their heads high. I won't
step out of that line or push my son out.
Give me a kid with braces and glasses
who gets C-pluses in social studies,
makes his mom a dustpan in metal shop,
washes dishes part-time, goes to trade school,
and marries a nice girl who's overweight
but has a pretty smile, then settles down,
keeps a steady job, and gives me grandkids.
I don't want front-row seats to some snooty
concert at Carnegie Hall. Just let me
sit on the porch with him, drinking a Bud,
catching the Royals on the radio,
watching his kids splash in the plastic pool
I bought 'em for ten bucks at Ben Franklin.

Neither need have worried that the other's
dream would be fulfilled. Mother's ended first,
when Kodiak was ten, at the train tracks
with a friend, taking turns driving a spike
with a sledge hammer Kodiak borrowed
from father's shop. When his friend missed, it broke
six bones in Kodiak's hand. The bones healed,
but not the nerves to his little finger.
Father's dreams lasted longer, but ended
more decisively. In a summer job
at sixteen, a gofer on a road crew
helping build a bridge across Cain's Mill Creek,
Kodiak died. The clutch on the crane slipped,
and its hook fell through his borrowed hard hat.
The funeral home kept the casket closed.
At mother's request, they played Mendelssohn.

Kodiak

God's sure hearing seconds a sense of smell
as sharp as a shark's. God's powerful jaws
dwarf his primitive brain. God stays hungry.
Human bones have been found in his gut,
engorged with tin cans, car tires, twisted parts
of metal grocery carts. God noses things
he wants to know. His shagreened underbelly
grists the skin of anyone he grazes.

2.

Kenai

In winter, my brothers and I would ski
in our houseshoes across the red shag carpet.
The tiny spark when we touched each other

made our fingers tingle; touching father
hurt. It sounded loud, like a cap-gun's pop,
and left a residue of smoke like the streak
on a finger passed through a candle flame.

My father functioned as our first remote:
his merely nearing the TV turned it off.
He wore his hair greased down his whole life
because when it was dry it stood on end.
When rain threatened, my brothers and I
were not allowed even to stand near him.

Not that lightning waited for a storm.
Nothing so predictable would threaten,
nothing so obedient speak for God.
Besides, physical proximity made
no difference: blood kinship, not sharing
his roof or holding his hand, cost us our lives.

Alaska

A tornado took my brother Kenai
but it left my father's shop intact.
It leveled the house, leveled the whole block,
leveled what it left of our family,
but my father's shop remained intact.
It took down trees that saw the Civil War,
destroyed the school my father's father built,
but left my father's flimsy shop intact.

Only McKinley would speak of that storm.
He had gone with Kenai after supper
to see if the Stern brothers three doors down
could come out and play. Mr. Stern said no,
a storm was on the way, they should go home.
He paced a front yard littered with toys,
but what he picked up, McKinley recalled,

was a red tricycle with red streamers
and white fenders already pocked with rust.

    Mother had spent the day cleaning, and wore
her cotton garden scarf, folded and tied,
as a headband. She had swept, mopped, vacuumed,
even washed the woodwork. Her face shone, flushed
red as phlox, and her yellow latex gloves
lay limp on the lip of the tub. Outside,
the air felt thin, as if they were closer
by 12,000 feet to God, as if some
bigger being than themselves claimed the same air,
leaving too little to fill their small lungs.
As McKinley recalled it, power failed
on only our side of the street. No one
thought to use the car radio. He heard
the K.C. Southern pass at 6:15.
He remembered Kenai bringing the bird
outside in its cage, asking our mother,
his voice small, *What about Forget-Me-Not?*
He remembered pieces of paper,
he said, soaring high in the air, like birds.

    The contractor's death had left the next lot
vacant, only a narrow, hip-deep trench
to foretell the foundation of a house.
The trench was muddy. Kenai had new boots.
McKinley said he could still see father
on one knee before fidgety Kenai,
fighting against a knot in the laces
while the eerie silence changed into noise.

    As a child, fishing with her grandfather,
mother had seen a tornado aloft,
so she recognized the roar. *God!* she cried,
and father picked up Kenai, boots still on,

carried him across the driveway, tossed him
at McKinley, already in the trench,
jumped in himself, and yelled, *Everyone down!*
Kodiak, the oldest, was at a friend's,
so Kenai and McKinley were to crouch
together holding hands while our father
covered Logan and our mother, pregnant
with Elias, covered Hamilton.
Kenai looked up, then pulled his hands away
to cover his eyes, blasted with debris.
McKinley said he had to brace himself
on the mud walls against being sucked out.
    The storm's roar sounded like sitting beneath
the trestle bridge when the K.C. Southern crossed,
magnified. When the tornado had passed,
our father pushed away debris fallen
across the trench, and they rose from the mud.
The car and our refrigerator rose
above strewn rubble where our house had been.
Father's shop stood, intact. Kenai was gone.
One of our cancelled mortgage checks was found
later, a hundred miles east. In the car
where mother had tossed him, Forget-Me-Not
survived, but no one saw Kenai again.

Kenai

Posted on fenceposts and phone poles God scans
the prairie grass with eyesight keen enough
to see field mice a quarter mile away.
God's rust-colored wings span four feet. Razored
talons indulge his appetite for flesh.

3.

McKinley

My father's fascination with Alaska,
a sun at summer solstice, never set.
He collected books, he clipped articles.
He knew the history, Gondwanaland
to ice age land bridge crossings, gold rushes
to tidal waves. He knew geography,
names of rivers, mountains, national parks;
he knew the life cycle of the salmon;
he knew blowholes and baleen, bald eagles,
bison, musk oxen, polar bears, caribou,
the range of a wolverine, the weight
a grizzly must gain in the short summer
before its long sleep; he knew wildflowers,
glaciers, islands, trees, annual snowfall,
migrating birds. We heard a hundred times
how he would homestead on the Yukon
were it not for us. Hunt moose in summer,
saw the frozen meat in winter. Travel
by dogsled and snowmobile and kayak.
Hear the howling of wolves and cold wind,
or the held-breath hush heard only in snow.
        Mother's daydreams adopted Florida.
Surrounded by hills, he wanted mountains;
living beside a lake, she longed for tides.
He wanted a cabin smothered in snow,
chimney smoking under the northern lights;
she a beachside bungalow, all its doors
and windows open to the ocean breeze.
Traveling by motorcycle, her chin
resting on father's shoulder, in the wind.

Shopping in Miami. White sand beaches
littered with seashells. Under umbrellas,
parents watching children play in the waves.
        We lived between Fairbanks and Key Biscayne,
taught to believe home meant someplace distant.

Alaska

At the moment my brother McKinley's car
left the road, his only living brother,
Seward, was listening to a record
on McKinley's headphones in their bedroom.
        When McKinley's car hit the walnut tree
that shoved its engine into the front seat,
his father was spraying primer over
a section of iron fence whose guilloche
entwined rearing bears and soaring eagles.
        The instant McKinley's head hit the windshield
his mother dropped the glass she was rinsing,
having come to the kitchen for milk
when a nightmare woke her from troubled sleep.
        In frozen air, his crushed radiator's
hissing drowned the whispers of snowflakes,
the only witnesses to his last breath.
While his sisters slept, he joined his brothers.

McKinley

God's broad footpads barely break the snow's crust.
White fur will not protect you, nor stillness:
her sense of smell will find you. She will stalk
until you panic, then end the chase soon,
when she snaps your brittle neck in her jaws.

4.

Logan

The tiny nod that dropped his welder's mask
over my father's face summarized him,
tipped his hat toward duty and hard work
and feeding his family, all he knew
of being a man. He sung wrought iron:
scores of fences, gates, ornamental work
to highlight gazebos and mailbox stands;
balusters and railings and struts, the kind
that once ornamented stylish porches,
now used for nothing but nostalgia.
He built the biggest wrought-iron business
in the five-state region, with customers
as far away as Tulsa and Lincoln.

    My father would not use a Mig welder.
Mig represented the progress he scorned:
fancy machines that made things easier
but not better. Mig offered improvement
only to those too lazy to master
the arc welder, but he could pull a bead
that looked soft, like fresh caulk or putty
smoothed by a thumb. Only touch revealed
the waves formed as molten metal cooled.
Those welded seams felt like his idea
of love: firm, straight, smooth. With an arc welder,
he said, a man knew when his work was right:
nothing had to be chipped, the flux peeled off
on its own as if in praise of good work.

    And work my father did, continually.
Except for short naps, I never saw him
asleep till I was thirteen. At bedtime,

if he was not tucking me in, I knew
I could look beyond the gravel drive
and see in the windows of his shop
the familiar flickering—like lightning—
of the welder. By the time I woke up
he would be at work already. Sometimes
he came to the house to sip juice and smile
while my brothers and I buttered our toast,
but more often we would stop in the shop
to say goodbye on our way to the bus.

Alaska

In my memory, *leukemia* stands
as the first name death was given, *Logan*
the first death took. In the month of my birth
he entered a remission that lasted
most of the magic five years that level
the odds of survival. I was a child;
I envied him the attention. No one
talked about my fifth birthday, only his
anniversary. One morning he woke
weak, didn't finish his breakfast. The next
he woke in the hospital. The doctors
gave their message to my parents clearly,
and they gave it clearly to us: Logan
would be leaving soon, and not coming back.
    Lucid enough to forego more treatment,
Logan learned what we ten taught our parents,
what only we the dead know: imagined death
threatens, experienced death liberates.
    The spinal taps, hair loss, and vomiting
happened before my birth; I remember
the white sheets stretched tight, i.v. tubes, machines,

the nurse who started crying in his room,
and that when he called me to him, holding
my hand, he told me to be a good girl
and a happy one, that my condition
came from his decision to live in me.
We dying must find another body,
he said. He and I were inseparable:
he would leave the others, but never me.

Logan

God's voice stays always almost audible:
coruscations in cold cloudtops below
must mean thunder in the thin air, muffled
by scarred plane windows, edges singed with frost,
through which sunlight ushers the tangerines
and lavenders of wave-lorn billows.

5.

Hamilton

A town of eight hundred people, Resolve
hugs Lake Resolution, in the Ozarks
two hours southeast of Kansas City.
Through metamorphosis from farming village
to retirement town, its population
has stayed constant, as if to verify
Socrates' last argument, about
the living being replaced by the dead.
The children of Resolve go to college
in Springfield or to work in Independence
and never come back, because you can cruise
the parking lots of the grocery store

and skating rink only so many times.
For every youth who leaves, a senior
from Little Rock or Kansas City comes
to settle into the "retirement village"
or buy a plywood cottage on the lake.
Even they don't stay. They drive off in pairs
in Winnebagos, blue Buicks in tow,
to visit the grandchildren in Fort Smith
or test the KOA in Estes Park
against the one in Virginia Beach.
        The two cafés in town have served a hunk
of meat and three too-salty sides since the Fall,
but when a Furr's moves in will disappear
as their owners' kids did decades ago.

Alaska

The year after Hamilton's accident,
the city council paved his school's playground,
but the gravel had done its work by then.
        If you lift someone from behind just right,
you can paralyze his diaphragm. Held
thus long enough, the victim will pass out.
At Resolution Elementary
no one took more pleasure in this knowledge
than Zachary Carlson, held back a year,
and just that much bigger and angrier
than anyone else in Hamilton's class.
        Short, skinny Hamilton's poor vision meant
thick glasses and a squint that showed his teeth,
and made him play weak gazelle for Zach.
The third time, with a teacher on the way
to disperse the crowd of kids, Zach lifted
a little and dropped him harder, for show.

Hamilton landed headfirst, and never
regained consciousness. The ambulance took
half an hour to arrive; the hospital
was out of his blood type, so they drove him
to Kansas City. He never awoke
from the coma he entered on the way.

Hamilton

Not Leviathan, but the unseen source
of his scars. Never-surfacing Satan,
chased sustenance to the one who must breathe.
Seducer to strict darkness and pressure.
Soft-bodied gripper with infinite arms.
To live, Leviathan must dive, called down,
knowing, to die one day in God's cold depths.

6.

Elias

On summer afternoons I would have walked
to the lake, watched minnows in the shallows,
imagining myself a scientist
peering past the pontoons of his prop plane
at the pod of whales below, would have felt
with my feet the sudsy green sapropel
in pockets along the shore, the rhythmic
slapping and sucking of small waves on mud
when a breeze kicks up, watched on stiller days
a great blue heron meditate the whole
waterscape into perfect watchfulness.
        I would have reveled in the walk itself,
a mile along the tracks to the tangent

where trains nearly touched the lake, that short path
barely one boy wide but perforating
the blackberried scrub that separated
built things from the woods that embraced the lake,
the crunch of Converse on gravel, the ties
my steps made regular when I walked, left
singular when I stopped. I would have loved
putting an ear to one rail, listening,
then standing by the tracks as a train passed,
watching the ties float, feeling earth tremble
the way the ground in Eden gave when God
wandered the garden. I would have savored
counting cars and hailing the caboose,
awaiting the brakeman's waving back.

  Mother, sleep. What withheld the world from me
and me from you, you could not have altered:
not the tornado, but what spoke through it.
  Even we who never lived, suffered.

Alaska

Some other world than this one made him smile:
Elias was hydranencephalic.
Our mother called him her little angel:
the halated, liquid globe of his skull
shone, a paper lantern, lit from the back.
It was not our world that made him smile,
but some other that transformed his pupils
into searchlights scanning a blank black lake.
Our mother called him her little angel,
and loved him with a love fated to fail,
the pristine love that only grief can make.
Whatever other world lent him his smile
foretold itself as landscape—blood vessels,

black winter trees, branched in the fluid sac.
Mother made his brothers call him angel
to train them for his inevitable
death. His brainstem, bereft, communicant
with some world other than ours, made his smile
its message to Mother, made him her angel.

Elias

Instantly, from some element rarer
than ours, clearer, with no revelations
more than long legs, twigs blent with the decay
and lutulence of our cluttered world (dense
with fallen things), after just eternity
enough of perfect stillness to dissolve
the memory of her wide wings' shadow,
God's snake-like neck and sharp beak strike,
and she swallows another soul whole.

7.

Seward

My father always smelled faintly of smoke,
not spent tobacco, or welded metal,
but tinge of singed hair. The soles of his feet
hurt all the time, as if they bore blisters,
and so did his palms. In front of his heart
on the burned spot, the hair never grew back.
    Electricity flows through your body
along the channels that conduct it best,
the nerves and oxygen-rich arteries,
so it always finds your heart and your brain:
that's why so many victims have seizures

or heart attacks. My father saw bright light
constantly, even when his eyes were closed,
just left of whatever he was facing.
His memory tilted. He remembered
word for word the script of a TV show
about Denali he had seen just once,
yet he often forgot his children's names,
and his own. The bathroom mirror scared him
sometimes, he said, with his own reflection,
unexpected, illegible. He stared hard
to recognize his image as himself.

Alaska

The note they found by Seward's bed the day
he did not wake recounted a nightmare
he must have had for years, since the morning
he saw what no one knew he had seen.
    I was walking along the railroad tracks
behind the house. The moon was bright enough
for me to see my feet, and I could hear
my shoes on the gravel at every step,
but the sights were out of sync with the sounds,
so I kept turning my head, looking back
to see if the footsteps I was hearing
were mine, or a stranger's following me.
When I looked ahead, even in the dark
I could see Juneau straddling a limb
on a tree beside the tracks. I could tell
it was going to break, that she would fall
and be hurt, so I panicked and started
running toward the house through the back yard,
which in the dream stretched out, and seemed in fact
to go on forever. I was trying

to yell for you, but my voice wouldn't work.
It sounded hoarse, cracked, and tiny, the voice
of someone sick awakened in the night
answering the phone. When you left the house
by the back steps, letting the screen slap shut,
you stepped into separate cars, neither
of them ours. I kept running toward you,
trying to yell, but nothing would come out.
Both cars started up, their headlights came on,
they backed around, then drove into the night.
You never saw me waving my arms.
I woke without saving Juneau, who still
sits clutching the limb even as it cracks.

Seward

God sings to himself at night, howls colder
than snow bending spruce limbs. God hunts in packs.
Circling you, reflecting back your fire's light,
his wild eyes shine, define a horizon,
a dozen level pairs of restless stars,
wary, hungrier than the woods are black.

8.

Juneau

A theology possessed of thunder
needs no throne, no garden, no three-in-one;
enthralled to fire, it needs no thurible.
    Sometimes it takes no more than the sun's heat
to compromise the pellicle between
warm, moist air and the cool, dry air above
to which it aspires. As the raptured air

expands and cools, its water vapor
condenses, forming a flat cloud base.
Warmed by the process of condensation,
the air, rising more rapidly, creates
a cloud tall enough to contain God.

 Lightning strikes the earth twenty million times
a year in the United States alone.
In only a few hundred of those strikes
does someone die for standing in the way.
Odds say you'll sooner be hit by a truck
or jump off a bridge or get skin cancer,
but lightning alone displays your death
as a casualty of the battle
between earth and sky, devil and god.

 Celestials themselves must fear lightning,
since it can streak not only down to earth
but also up to heaven. Above clouds,
lightning appears as red expanding disks
or as red pulses or cones of blue light.

 Heavens so charged imply a pantheon
of adversaries but no advocates.

Alaska

Juneau came back crying from the tracks
one day when she was five. Mother could not
get her to say why. She cried harder. *He said
he would hurt you and Daddy if I told.*
Mother cleaned her up. Futilely, father
followed his fury to the tracks, a length
of iron from the shop clutched in his fist.
They never called the sheriff. What would be
the point? No one noticed Seward's absence,
and no one noticed him when he returned.

One decade later, nearly to the day,
Juneau did not come back. She had gone out
with friends to an end-of-summer party,
promising to be back home by midnight.
This time my parents did call the sheriff,
after calling one of her friends at two
and learning the friend was already home.
Juneau had left with Jason Pederson,
a junior at her school, two grades ahead.
The sheriff found Jason's car at the lake,
empty. They searched the woods, they dragged the lake.
No sign. On the third anniversary
of her disappearance, my parents placed
a stone for her beside her brothers' graves.

Juneau

Let others, to whom the god of power
has not spoken, pray to the god of love.

9.

Aurora

Like other bodies, including earth, humans
generate an electrical charge
and a magnetic field, one to regulate
the heartbeat and make the neurons sing,
the other to navigate, as sea turtles,
birds, and generations of monarchs steer.
Some fish can generate a kilowatt.
My father's charge, though, was anomalous.
Some people can't wear a watch: their wrists
will not let it work. He couldn't walk outside
because the sky paid him too much attention.

As I speak, eighteen hundred thunderstorms
darken skies at places the world over.
In the time it takes to read this phrase,
more than one hundred lightning bolts will strike,
positive earth joined to negative sky,
often a nimbus cloud nine miles high.
Each will last one one-hundredth of a second,
but grow hot as the center of the sun.
Most will scar sites indifferent to us,
but some will mark houses, cows, ancient trees.
Some will create a rock called fulgurite,
vitrifying images of themselves
at their entry points into sandy soil.
    One of them is searching for my father.

Alaska

It started, her wasting away, older
sister by then grown younger than I was,
she who lived my youth as I lived her age,
it started with shifting her food around,
chicken hidden under sliced lettuce leaves
or beef given back, disguised as gristle,
peas folded into napkins, everything
cut into smaller and smaller pieces.
It started with feeding more to the dog,
serving others seconds from the kitchen,
and rising first to run the dishwater.
It started with learning to make desserts,
ever richer and more extravagant,
but eating smaller and smaller servings.
It started with such semaphores, such cries
for help, but none of us understood her
until too late. Our parents encouraged

what they first saw: she became generous
and helpful, she grew more active, she glowed.

Her aura soon faded. We shared a room,
so while I chased old age I watched her
turn herself back into a little girl.
Her breasts shrank back to nothing, her shoulders
and elbows and ribs hardened her, hunger
stopped her periods, her fingers and feet
stayed cold, soft down grew over her body.
She stopped sleeping. She paced around her bed
for hours: I fell asleep to her restless
motion, I woke to it in the morning.

At eighty pounds they hospitalized her.
The doctors used a feeding tube, but when
she was released, her habits still held her.
They tried to make her eat. Mother watched her
at every meal, so she turned to purging,
developing, as we later inferred,
the hypokalemia that killed her,
inducing sudden cardiac arrest.

Aurora

I who feared God's wrath died from his embrace.

10.

Alaska

I think I stole my father's sense of cold,
for his withholding my wedding to time.
He was struck again the morning after
I was conceived, and from that time forward
he and mother slept in separate beds

except in summer, when she could sleep without
sheet or blanket, as he slept all year round.
He felt in January wind as snow
at ten thousand feet must feel in June sun.
My father shoveled snow in summer shorts.
Each December 12th he climbed the ladder
to string Christmas lights, dressed only in jeans
and a T-shirt, whatever the weather,
regardless of mother's embarrassment.
Everyone saw him: neighbors, the mailman,
people driving by. Our schoolmates teased me
and my sisters, so we pleaded with him
to wear a coat, not to appear outside
exactly as he did in, but nothing
would stop him. Nothing short of lightning will.

  When I die, my parents will look around
at the house, at the train tracks, at the sky,
at my father's rusting shop, my mother's
old upright, the flower garden, the lake.
They will call God by all the names they know,
Kodiak, Logan, Aurora, Alaska,
Hard Work, Daily Practice, Grown from Cuttings,
A Seam like Putty, Seed for the Sparrows,
but since God never speaks when spoken to,
they'll trade the car for a motorcycle,
and lock the house, and head to Florida.

  Q: In what state does lightning strike
twice as often as in any other?
A: Florida, with six strikes per square
kilometer per year, far more than
the three that Missouri and Kansas average.

  •

Of the three brothers old enough to know
Eden, before the summer of lightning,

only McKinley lived long enough
to describe the garden I never knew:
That summer things began to go wrong.
Before that year, the world pretended
to be a proud, benevolent parent.
When we did our chores—and our family
always does its chores—the world gave us
our allowance and a maternal hug
or a paternal nod of approval
at least. It cooked our breakfast while we dressed,
waited for us at the door after school,
interrupted its work to play with us,
and at bedtime made up stories for us
in which the character most like ourselves
slew the dragon and earned a grateful kiss.

My life made me tell a different story.
One does not discover the absurd,
said sad Camus, *without being tempted*
to write a manual of happiness.
This absurd immanual discovered me.
I am Alaska, father's favorite,
child of my parents' old age, love child,
their Isaac, their Benjamin, their last hope,
last left standing, next in line to fall.
I clutched a rattle of grief seeds until
time pried my fingers from it one by one.
We ten got our thunderbolts; each of us
heard the voice of God. I alone escaped
sufficiently intact to tell the tale.

I am my one mutated gene, I am
progeria, from the Greek for *hurry*
and *don't expect much*, I am the Latin
tempus fugit, which means *I never got*
even the chance you had to fail at love.

I am the syndrome named for Progeric
Hutchinson and T. Fugitive Gilford,
I am a cold clinical description
that begins with *a cyanotic tinge*
in infancy, drones through retardation
of bodily growth, crowded dentition,
pyriform thorax, gibbous abdomen,
beaked nose, micrognathia, and ends in
cardiovascular or cerebral
complications bring death sometime between
the ages seven and twenty-seven.
I am a body four times my own age.

    I am the Lichtenberg's flowers that mark
my father's skin, the thriving Russian sage
and coreopsis and black-eyed Susan
my mother tends in place of her children,
nine bunches of daisies that once a year
stand above my brothers' and sisters' graves,
one more, blooming already, meant for me.

    No one refuses God more doggedly
than I, no one has been offered more gifts
or had more denied her, no one has seen
more people fall, no one has lived a life
shorter, more absurd, or happier than mine.
God's gift of death came wrapped in foreknowledge.
Only we who can detect our dying,
observe its progress, and give it a name
grant its identity with our living,
not as mirror or twin, and certainly
not as opposite: my death *is* my life.

•

I wanted to know God until I did.
I wanted to be chosen until I was.

THE PROPHETS

Who sows the wind shall reap the whirlwind.
Sun shall turn to bile, moon turn to blood.
The great houses all shall come to an end.

Who sows the wind shall reap the whirlwind.
They have set a trap who ate your bread.
When sun turns to bile and moon to blood
mariners will cry to their gods in fear.
Houses of ivory shall be destroyed
and mountains melt like wax near fire.

Who sows the wind shall reap the whirlwind.
Guard the towers. Watch the road. Gird your loins.
Sun shall thicken to bile, moon to blood.
Fig trees shall wither, no fruit grow on vines,
and the greatest houses come to an end,
their acreage strangled by thistle.
Who will set a trap will eat your bread.
Strong horses with their riders shall fall,
and sailors implore the waves in fear.
Gods babble and diviners always lie.
High mountains melt like wax near fire.
I may open doors, but not to the sky.

Guard the towers, watch the road, gird your loins.
The brave riders of horses shall fall,
the fig tree wither, and drought blast the vines.
The gods babble to diviners, who lie
while earth succumbs to the thistle.
I open doors, but none to the sky.

Though their horses be strong, riders shall fall.
Gods babble and all diviners lie:
I will open no doors to the sky.

Synopsis

According to H.

Many others having presumed
  to tender account
of how what had to happen did,
  taking care to keep
intact the best testimony
  they could wrest from those
who say they saw what we all wish
  we could say we'd seen,
I felt obliged, Theophilus,
  to pass along this
I love of what I can't believe.

The Mother of the Mother of God

Anna's sighs drew her eyes upward.
Spying in tangled laurel limbs between herself and heaven
a sparrow's nest, she sang to summon the angel.

I was born to be hazed and cursed,
harried from the house of worship.
I am not like the birds of the air
that brood over hatchlings until they fly.
I am no doe, nose to the breezes,
ears raised, afraid for her fern-hidden fawn,
no sun-warmed tidal pool
teeming with algae, urchin, starfish, crab.
Not a fire from which ash flies
to nourish next year's wheat in the neighbor's field.

What I bear, I bear not as a child but as a gift.

From Mary's Childhood

When the priest placed her on the third step of the altar
God graced her with grace and she danced her praise.
Doted on as doves are doted on, desert be damned,
she ate, when she ate, from the hand of an angel.

One Sparrow

Until he clapped his hands we could not fly,
but all we know now we already knew
from the moment his fingers touched the clay.

He talked to himself, narrated his play,
named all twelve of us. All we could do
was wait 'til his clapped hands taught us to fly.

We did wait, heard that old man scold the boy,
would have held our breaths had we the lungs to,
but 'til his fingers touched, we were still clay.

Making us had kept his Sabbath holy:
birds out of clay supersedes any law,
and we knew when he clapped his hands we'd fly.

I was the third made, thrilled with my body,
thrilled soon to fly, but thrilled most that I *saw*
from the moment his fingers touched the clay.

The men were amazed and went away
to tell others, who would doubt it was true
that when the boy clapped his hands we could fly,
though *we* knew the moment he touched the clay.

Zacchaeus the Teacher, Shamed

This child speaks from some other world.
I beg you to take him away.

He knows letters as we cannot.
His gaze burns, too severe to bear.
Please, my brother, take him away.

He knows letters we do not know,
and how to spell out worlds with them.
I cannot understand his speech.

Who knows what belly bore this boy
born before our brown earth was born,
whose words neither begin nor end.
I understood speech, until his.

I have been deceiving myself,
thinking I could teach anyone.
Take the boy away, my brother.
How could I even meet his eye?
Whatever he is—angel, god—
I do not know what I should say.

Before our earth was born, he was.
He knows how letters spell our world.
I beg you, take this boy away
before I burn in his strict gaze.

I know not what belly bore him.
It is not mine to say his name.
What would I call him? angel? god?
How should I look him in the face?

I have fooled myself until now.
The child speaks of another world
more our world than our world itself.
I dare not look him in the face.
What begins, begins in his words.

Which of us understands his speech?
Who has a gaze severe enough?
Who knows our world the way he knows?

My fear begs you take him away.
This I understand from his words:
I have fooled myself until now.

Beatitudes

Once the crowd grew, he withdrew to the rise.
To aspirants who followed him he said:
Replete are the breathless; theirs are the skies.
Replete, those who grieve, who must be consoled.
Replete, who stake no claim; all earth is theirs.
Replete, the fairness-famished; be they fed.
Replete, those who give mercy to others.
Replete, the transparent; seen, they see God.
Replete, those who make peace where there were wars.
Replete, all who suffer for doing good.
Replete you will be despite those jealous
of your repletion, themselves depleted.
Savor their slanders. Their forgotten fathers
slandered the prophets whose truths we remember.

Light

All our eyes saw, we saw as God sees it.
Not the glow that is God, but all it lit.

Miracles

About a beggar blind from birth they asked,
Who bears the blame, this man or his parents?
He replied, *Seek not cause but occasion.*
He spat, made a paste of dust and spittle,
molded it over the blind man's eyelids,
and sent him to wash in Siloam's pool.

    •

Even as waves broke over the boat,
lightning showed him still asleep in the stern,
and they marveled at one not subject to storms.

    •

When the crowd found him on the other shore,
he said to them, *You seek me not because
my words sustain you but because I gave
you back more bread than you had brought. Go,
find bread within yourselves, among yourselves.*

Parables

What he said, he said only as parables.
Why light a lamp, he asked, but then hide it?
Placed on a table, it lights the whole room,
and those with sight see all that can be seen.

    •

A man prepared a feast and sent for friends,
but each sent back elaborate regrets:
*Just bought some property, need to check it out.
New BMW, need to break it in.*

My new lover's in town, just for the weekend.
So he had his help bring in from the streets
homeless persons, disfigured, disabled, blind,
who gladly filled his home and shared his food.

    •

A vintner with two children said to her son,
Put in some work today in the vineyard.
Sure, he said, but didn't leave the couch all day.
To her daughter she gave the same charge. *No way,*
the daughter said, but later went and worked.

    •

A wife was beaten often by her husband.
Every week or two, a few more bruises.
The other soccer moms tried not to notice.
Her pastor urged her to obedience.
The tattooed punk in the next cubicle
found out how to get her and her daughter
into a shelter, took time off from work
to drive them there in his old car, and gave
the shelter something from his check each month.

    •

One woman led her Sunday school class in prayer:
Thank you, God, for giving us salvation
and for promising us eternal life.
Another, alone in her room, not knowing
who to call on, wept: *Help me, please, help me.*

    •

If he had known in advance the thieves' plans,
his home would not have been broken into.

    •

A dying man willed his son the fallow field
his father had willed him. The son sold the land.
The buyer, plowing it in spring, unearthed a cache
long buried there, and now owns much more land.

    •

A moving company was short on help.
Going early to the unemployment line
the manager hired hands to help for the day.
He went again mid-morning, then again
at lunch, and one more time mid-afternoon.
At the end of the day, he had H.R.
pay each a hundred bucks. Those hired first complained.
Friend, he countered to their spokesperson, *what's wrong?*
I've been fair and honest with you, paying
the full amount we agreed to. Why begrudge
my being generous with someone else?

          •

Though its seed be tiny, mustard, tended,
grows large enough for birds to nest in.

          •

A widow whose husband had given her
over the years a dozen different rings
lost one of them. For a week she moved chairs,
emptied the vacuum cleaner bag, lost sleep,
cleaned cabinets, pulled clothes from dresser drawers.
When she found the ring, she had her best friends
in for dinner to help her celebrate.

          •

A rancher had two sons. The younger asked
for his inheritance—he wanted out.
The father sold half his land and half his stock.
The son moved to the city, tried college,
drank a lot, played pool and poker, slept late,
went to parties, met women, bought them nice clothes,
drove a Viper for a while, then a 'Vette.
When the money ran out, he washed dishes,
did gofer work at a construction site,
sold his car to pay off credit card debt,

and figured out he'd be better back at home:
at least the ranch hands have a roof and get fed.
He hitchhiked home, and hadn't hit the door
before his father tearfully embraced him.
The son had prepared his speech: *I screwed up.*
I'm not your son. Hire me back as a hand.
The father got him decent jeans and boots,
had half the county in to share a steer.
The older son was angry: *I helped here*
the whole time he was throwing money at cars
and whiskey and whores, and you never gave
a party for me. The father replied,
Son, we've shared work and weather. All I have
is yours. But it's right to celebrate now:
your brother who was lost to us has been found;
my son who was dead lives with us again.

·

All he told them, he told as parables.
A woman, he said, mixed just a little yeast
in with the flour, and the whole loaf rose.

Agrapha

Near me, near fire. Far from me, orphaned in darkness and cold.

Small thing, easy thing, to forfeit one's soul.

One proud man can clutter continents.

Trouble itself is far from God; a soul in trouble is near God.

A man missed the call, listening for his name.

It doesn't matter whether you *believe* I speak from another world.

Kerygma

Even during the watch of Elijah
there walked widows enough across a land
starved by stingy skies, crusted in parched soil,
but he was sent to only one of them,
a widow in Sidon named Sarepta.
Of all the lepers in Elisha's time
only Naaman the Syrian was healed.

·

Is it so hard to understand
that corruption does not enter
from outside but arises from within?

·

How can you fail to grasp
that when I speak of bread
I do not mean bread?

·

I tell you, Elijah *has* come.

Mercies

They said to him, *The law insists on stones.*
Ignoring them, he knelt, scribbling in dust.
They said again, *The law insists on stones.*
His finger kept moving across the dust.

·

Simon, see this woman.
You gave me no water for my feet,
but she washed them with her tears
and wiped them with her own hair.
You gave me no kiss to welcome me,
but she has not stopped kissing my feet.

You did not anoint my head
but she has anointed my feet.
To *her* I say, *Take respite. Be whole.*
You are reunited with yourself.

Hymn

Having gathered us together he said, *Before I am handed over,*
join me in a hymn to the law that is law. Prepare to embrace
what awaits us. So we circled him and he said, *Respond amen to me.*

I will grow, and I will feed what grows. Amen.
I will imprison, and be imprisoned. Amen.
I will free, and be freed. Amen.
I will burn and burn, and I will be burned. Amen.
I will bear the burden borne by what bears me. Amen.
I will pierce, and be pierced. Amen.

  Grace that gives grace does so by dancing.

I would drown, had I not drowned already. Amen.
I would let go the hand that holds me, had I not fallen already. Amen.
I would forfeit my food to the hungry, had I not already starved. Amen.
I would carry earth's curvature, were not my own horizon so near. Amen.
I would singe treetops, blown branch to branch, were I not already ash. Amen.
I would stare down the sun, were I not already blind. Amen.
I would die for you, were I not already dead. Amen.

  What grace cannot give cannot be given.
  Dancing gives what even grace withholds.

When I listen, what I hear replaces love. Amen.
When I sing, my voice replaces faith. Amen.
When I dance, my body replaces grief. Amen.
I will listen if you will sing. Amen.

I will sing if you will dance. Amen.
I tell you the earth's movement is a dance. Amen.
I tell you knowledge is not knowledge, but dancing is. Amen.
Hope is not hope, but dancing is. Amen.
Time is not fire, but dancing is the stars. Amen.
God scorns sacrifices of barley and goats
but offer your hand and God may dance with you. Amen. And amen.

Passions

Peter, James, and John, Sleeping: You watch for betrayal, we betray it.

Sarra: You must kill the lawless to reveal the law.

Judas: Lead him away, for his own safety.

Malchos: The literal is the lesser loss.

Peter: Now neither of us knows him, you nor I.

Pilate: Every crowd seeks to harm itself.

Barabbas: I acted; he spoke, a more heinous crime.

Gestas: My petty claims still curse your pompous ones.

The Centurion: Where should we see God if not in a death?

Joseph of Arimathea: Light cannot be buried in a cave.

Veronica: On this thin fabric, my blood, his image.

Mary Magdalene, Mary the Mother of James, & Salome: Words sound different from an angel.

Cleopas: Did not our very viscera burn?

Conclusion

Beyond what's here, much more.
Of the word that writes itself,
not books enough, nor world.

Protevangelium

I, Harvey, wrote this history
    here in the mountains
while tumult raged in the desert.
    I had to see snow,
though which evoked this history—
    the desert, the snow—
I don't know. I praise what I can,
    as I am able,
and solicit a miracle
    beyond my desert:
from my emptiness, history,
    from history, grace.

The Letters

Creation submits to futility.
My innocence has not acquitted me.

Creation bows before futility:
we can do nothing against the truth.
Innocence will never acquit me.
Truth has made me your enemy.

Creation embodies futility:
try to find out what would satisfy God.
Still, my innocence tries to acquit me
so no third grief can shadow the second.
Against the truth we can do nothing.
Why live as if we belonged in the world?
Truth has made you my enemy.
Those who drink drink at night, those who sleep sleep.

Creation sounds futility's laughter.
Some laugh when they drink, some laugh in their sleep.
My innocence acquits me of nothing:
the mystery of lawlessness at work,
a truth I can do nothing against.
Some people's sins lead, others' sins follow.
Truth has made me your enemy.
Rekindle the divine flame within you:
try to learn what would make you a god.
All with me here send you greetings,
sure no third grief will shadow the second.
One thing more—prepare a guest room for me
to live as if I belonged in the world.
Change in the priesthood changes the law.

Those who drink drink at night, then sleep, sleep.
Even demons believe, and shudder
not at lawlessness but at mystery.
Sustain yourself with fear through your exile.
Some people's sins lead, others' follow.
God spared not even birds when they sinned,
so rekindle the divine flame in you.
Love neither the world nor what is in it.
All with me here send you warning
of the deceivers who riddle the world.
One more time prepare a guest room for me:
I will come and go as quickly as birds.
Change in the priesthood changes the law.
Stars never ask how darkness was made.

First change the priesthood, then change the law
from hate the world to hate what is in it.
Even demons believe, and shudder
at the liars who populate the world.
Your fellows live on fear in their exile:
nourish them with fear worthy of God,
who would not spare birds if they sinned.
Light does not spare even wandering stars.

Love neither the world nor things in the world:
reject them in a way worthy of God.
Many deceivers have entered the world,
bringing darkness in which even stars hide.

Send them on in a way worthy of birds,
wandering stars for whom darkness was made.

Calendologium

Before the Day of Trust, the Year of Terror

But that my having fallen came first,
I had not known to call *falling*

this feeling of following grainy shades
into gray, waving for want of wings,

or *fog* this silent summoning,
a city sunk whole under a sea.

Who would watch waves must lean into wind.
They wind up lean who long want rain.

If not for waiting, why have we mouths?
If not for failing to fly, why fingers?

Before the Day of Peace, the Year of Occupation

First we see the mothers composed
mostly of smoke, only later

hear them hum above their drowned daughters
lullabies that rename them *Debris*.

Winding sheets assert themselves white
first against a wispscape of ash,

second inside—no, *as*—the hush
of shroud-white birds innocent of song

fleeing their own tailfeathers, wronged black
by too-late flight from too-fast flame.

Before the Day of Hope, the Year of Spillage

Constellations nippling the night sky
mirror, as joint-mapped mythic monsters,

their mundane, flightless sisters,
islands risen molten from the sea.

Smog subdues this city, softens it
as oil muffles black the clatter

of rounded rocks, as plastic
silences the albatross. Glass

still reflects but, shattered, scans heaven
and nether, rather than horizon.

Before the Day of Innocence, the Year of Flood

Another locus, this, of *well why not*,
where sandbags sag useless, lightpoles lean.

List, o list. Kalmunai, Kamala,
Unawatuna, Cuddalore,

Nagapattinam. Multiply, increase.
On fish death forces rising, not falling.

Of humans, none knows worse thirst than one
afloat on a flood under circling birds.

In lieu for now of home, this raft
will have to do, or that blanket.

Before the Day of Gifts, the Year of Famine

Of wings there may be no census,
but which, their number or their swirling,

enforces on spring corn summer husk?
If there were enough of me,

why would I need to swim to cross the sea?
We clutch at mud to mimic those

buried under it. Open palms ask
what otherwise we don't know how to.

He hears himself hear his worship when—
only when—it shushes her weeping.

Before the Day of Reconciliation, the Year of Drought

Why shock what you can crucify?
Flames feign wings to force the burning to fly.

Strict ratio, if not cause and effect:
one infant hand grips its mother's chapped lips,

one father sews his own lips shut.
Even the thirsty weep water,

even windblown sand elicits it.
A human shadow across carved stone

will assume, if not the song
at least the silhouette of a bird.

VALEDICTION

What insistence, where, casts such a shadow?
What threat set these birds to waving goodbye?
Is sight truth coming in through the window

or going out? Where will these scared birds go?
What fear there chase them back to this place? Why?
When? What *sol* cast these migrating shadows?

What they repent must be something they know
that we don't, who only *look* at the sky
while we listen for truth through a window.

Birds bested questions generations ago;
now they say their valedictions and fly
as soon as cloudlight lengthens their shadows.

Even inside a room, shadows may grow,
may portend to us what they signify
to birds beyond thought, beyond this window.

What force mandates light above, dark below?
Confines us, frees birds to fly? Do they cry
to us, or each other? Whose is this shadow?
What truth waves us goodbye at this window?

Books from Etruscan Press

So Late, So Soon: New and Selected Poems | Carol Moldaw
Venison | Thorpe Moeckel
Incident Light | H. L. Hix
Peal | Bruce Bond
The Disappearance of Seth | Kazim Ali
Toucans in the Arctic | Scott Coffel
Synergos | Roberto Manzano
Lies Will Take You Somewhere | Sheila Schwartz
Legible Heavens | H. L. Hix
A Poetics of Hiroshima | William Heyen
Saint Joe's Passion | J. D. Schraffenberger
American Fugue | Alexis Stamatis
Drift Ice | Jennifer Atkinson
The Widening | Carol Moldaw
Parallel Lives | Michael Lind
God Bless: A Political/Poetic Discourse | H. L. Hix
Chromatic | H. L. Hix (National Book Award finalist)
The Confessions of Doc Williams & Other Poems | William Heyen
Art into Life | Frederick R. Karl
Shadows of Houses | H. L. Hix
The White Horse: A Colombian Journey | Diane Thiel
Wild and Whirling Words: A Poetic Conversation | H. L. Hix
Shoah Train | William Heyen (National Book Award finalist)
Crow Man | Tom Bailey
As Easy As Lying: Essays on Poetry | H. L. Hix
Cinder | Bruce Bond
Free Concert: New and Selected Poems | Milton Kessler
September 11, 2001: American Writers Respond | William Heyen

Founded in 2001 with a generous grant from the Oristaglio Foundation, Etruscan Press is a non-profit cooperative of poets and writers working to produce and promote books that nurture the dialogue among genres, achieve a distinctive voice, and reshape the literary and cultural histories of which we are a part.

ETRUSCAN IS PROUD OF SUPPORT RECEIVED FROM

Wilkes University

Youngstown State University

The Wean Foundation

The Ohio Arts Council

The Stephen & Jeryl Oristaglio Foundation

Nin & James Andrews Foundation

Council of Literary Magazines and Presses

Ruth H. Beecher Foundation

Bates-Manzano Fund

New Mexico Community Foundation

etruscan press
www.etruscanpress.org

Etruscan Press books may be ordered from

Consortium Book Sales and Distribution
800-283-3572
www.cbsd.com

Small Press Distribution
800-869-7553
www.spdbooks.com

Etruscan Press is a 501(c)(3) nonprofit organization.
Contributions to Etruscan Press are tax deductible
as allowed under applicable law.
For more information, a prospectus,
or to order one of our titles,
contact us at etruscanpress@gmail.com.